Daily
Meditations

The Great Virtues

Daily Meditations

The Great Virtues

Rev. James Alberione, S.S.P., S.T.D.

Translated by
the Daughters of St. Paul

ST. PAUL EDITIONS

NIHIL OBSTAT:
    Rev. Timothy J. Shea
    Censor
IMPRIMATUR:
    ✠ Most Rev. Bernard F. Law, D.D.
    Archbishop of Boston

Library of Congress Cataloging in Publication Data
Alberione, James, 1884-1971.
    Daily meditations.

Translation of: Brevi meditazioni per ogni giorno
dell'anno.
    1. Meditations.   I. Title.
BX2185.A3513   1985   242'.2   85-8241

The Scripture quotations in this publication are from the
Revised Standard Version Bible (modified form), Catholic Edi-
tion, copyrighted © 1965 and 1966 by the Division of Christian
Education of the National Council of the Churches of Christ in
the U.S.A., and used by permission.

Scripture verses designated New American Bible (NAB)
were taken from: *The New American Bible,* © 1970, used
herein by permission of the Confraternity of Christian Doctrine, copyright owner.

ISBN 0-8198-1810-0c
       0-8198-1811-9p

Cover credits: DSP; Gordon Alves, bottom right

Printed in the U.S.A., by the Daughters of St. Paul
50 St. Paul's Ave., Boston, MA 02130

The Daughters of St. Paul are an international congregation of
women religious serving the Church with the communications
media.

CONTENTS

Preface

I present these brief meditations to very busy people and to uncomplicated persons who incessantly and daily seek the food "which does not perish, but which is nourishment for everlasting life."

Every meditation contains, in brief, enough material to satisfy even those persons who devote themselves to meditation for a longer period of time, and who desire to investigate the topics more deeply.

The purpose of these meditations is to live Jesus, the Divine Master, who declared Himself to be the Way, the Truth and the Life. Therefore, every meditation indicates: the way to follow in order to walk behind Jesus Christ, the truths which He taught and which are to be believed, and the supernatural life in Christ which is to be lived.

The reader will be helped to fulfill the first great commandment, "...You shall love the Lord your God with all your heart, and with all your soul, and with all your mind, and with all your strength" (Mark 12:30). He will live in Christ, our Way, Truth and Life. He will be guided by Mary, who is Mother, Teacher and Queen of all who want to live "*in Christ and in the Church.*"

The Author

Meditation

Meditation has as its goal the strengthening of the will and the reconfirmation of good resolutions.

In meditation it is well to return often to the eternal truths and the doctrine of Jesus Master, Way, Truth and Life, as it is contained in the Gospels and in outstanding commentaries.

Meditation should never be reduced to a simple instruction of the mind or to spiritual reading. The major part of the time should be devoted to reflection, contrition, resolution and prayer. Thus, if one sets aside a half hour for meditation, about fifteen minutes should be spent in these acts.

Meditation has three parts besides the preparatory prayer and the prayer of thanksgiving.

The preparatory prayer consists in placing oneself in the presence of God, asking His light and the grace to derive firm and effective resolutions.

In the first part, the topic of the meditation is read with its brief development, or one may pause over a particular fact or mystery to contemplate it. In this part it is especially the mind that is exercised. The Divine Master enlightens with His moral and practical truths.

Often persons already experienced in meditation contemplate with simplicity a mystery, an episode from the life or passion of Jesus Christ, a practical maxim or one of the eternal truths. The soul enjoys the beauty, usefulness and necessity of following what the Divine Master teaches. It delights in the life of union with God and feels a foretaste of the reward promised by our Lord to His faithful servants, to those who love generously.

In the second part the will especially comes into play, with intense desire to sanctify one's life and to follow Jesus, who precedes us on the path to heaven. Acts of desire are made, as well as reflection or examination of conscience on the past, sorrow for sins and resolutions for the future.

In the third part prayer is necessary. One asks for the grace of perseverance, for the grace that what has not yet been accomplished because of weakness will be possible, easy and joyful through an abundance of divine assistance.

"O God, You know that our confidence is not based on human actions. Mercifully grant us, through the intercession of St. Paul, Apostle of the Gentiles, protection against all adversity. Through Christ our Lord. Amen."

Here various prayers may be recited, such as the Our Father, the Hail Mary, the Glory, some mystery of the rosary, the "Come, Holy Spirit," the "Soul of Christ," or Psalm 51 (the Miserere).

The final prayer consists in thanksgiving for God's assistance, an offering of the resolutions and a brief petition to be firm in keeping them.

Prayer Before Meditation

Rekindle the thought of God's presence and say:
O Jesus, Divine Master, I believe with lively faith that You are present here before me. I adore You with all my heart; I humble myself before You and ask pardon for the many and grave displeasures I have given You, my supreme Good. I resolve to die rather than to offend You again. Enlighten my mind; move my heart; give me the grace to derive good fruit from this meditation. Speak, O Lord, Your servant is listening. O Mary, my Mother and Teacher, my guardian angel and St. Paul the Apostle, pray for me.

Prayer After Meditation

I thank You, O Jesus Master, for the light which You have given me in this meditation. Pardon me all the faults and defects which I have committed during it.

I offer You the resolution I have made to amend this defect...and imitate You in the virtue of.... I ask You the grace to put into practice what I have resolved to do....

Mary, Queen of the Apostles, pray for me and unite your intercessions to my petitions before your Divine Son.

St. Paul the Apostle, pray for me.

The Great Virtues

"You shall love the Lord your God...with all your strength."   —Mark 12:30

FAITH—I

"Now faith is the assurance of things hoped for, the conviction of things not seen. For by it the men of old received divine approval. By faith we understand that the world was created by the word of God, so that what is seen was made out of things which do not appear."

—Hebrews 11:1-3

1. Faith is a theological virtue infused into our hearts by God. It helps us firmly believe the truths revealed by God and taught to us by the Church. We believe through the aid of divine grace—not because we understand the truths; we believe because they are revealed to us by God, who cannot be mistaken and cannot deceive us. St. Paul sums up everything in a few words: "Faith is the assurance of things hoped for, the conviction of things not seen" (Hebrews 11:1).

First of all, we believe in God and we believe God. Then, we believe the truths revealed by God to man. By divine and Catholic faith we are to believe all that is contained in Scripture and Tradition and which the Church proposes for the belief of the faithful, through either solemn or ordinary teaching. The Church alone is the true teacher of faith. To her alone and always, men can and are to entrust themselves entirely and with complete confidence, as children trust their mothers. Throughout the centuries, the Church has explained her doctrine to the faithful with ever greater clarity. She has condemned errors and defined truths solemnly. However, she has never proposed new truths or dogmas. All that she teaches she draws from the Revelation of which she is the guardian, witness and interpreter. We are more certain of the truths of faith than we are of the truths which we know by reason, or of the things we see with our own eyes!

2. Faith is the greatest good. It is the beginning of eternal salvation, the foundation and root of justification and grace. "Without faith it is impossible to please him. For whoever would draw near to God must believe that he exists and that he rewards those who seek him" (Hebrews 11:6).

The Divine Master teaches: "...he who does not believe will be condemned" (Mark 16:16). Therefore, everyone is obliged to accept the teachings of faith and submit to believing them, in order to receive the gift of divine grace. At least once in a while, every Christian ought to make positive acts of faith, but this is especially true at the point of death, in dangers and in temptations against faith.

3. Christians are obliged to instruct themselves, and pastors of souls should teach catechism and give instructions and sermons.

Instruction is necessary in order to receive the sacraments and defend oneself against the countless errors widespread in the world today. Instruction is also necessary in order to unite oneself always better to Jesus Christ with one's mind and to deserve to prepare for the eternal vision of God.

Parents, tutors, educators, teachers, employers, etc., are bound to provide for religious education programs according to their positions.

Reflection—Do I have faith? Do I try to learn more about the truths of faith? Do I think of instructing others?

Resolution—I have to listen to or read the Word of God. Even if I already know what is necessary, this practice will nourish my faith.

Prayer—Lord, help me to understand how useful and necessary it is for me to meditate on You and Your divine truths. May I know You! This is the foundation and beginning of holiness. I will love You more and know You better. If I penetrate Your teachings more, I will serve You more faithfully. Study and meditation of sacred things are the most necessary, the most useful, the most perfect, and the most refreshing to the spirit.

Give me, O divine Spirit, a hunger and thirst for Your divine wisdom, the true food of my soul. The soul does not live on bread, but on the truth which comes from the mouth of God.

FAITH—II

"God is light and in him is no darkness at all. If we say we have fellowship with him while we walk in darkness, we lie and do not live according to the truth; but if we walk in the light, as he is in the light, we have fellowship with one another, and the blood of Jesus his Son cleanses us from all sin."   —1 John 1:5-7

1. Faith is the light which illuminates man's way towards heaven. Through it the Christian is distinguished from the philosopher, just as reason distinguishes man from animal. The knowledge that comes from Revelation is more perfect, more lofty and more certain than the knowledge acquired by the intellect or through the senses. Faith makes us sharers in God's wisdom and unites us to Him. Through faith the light by which God knows Himself becomes our light; the wisdom of God, our wisdom; His mind, our mind; His life, our life. Faith is the fount of light for the mind, strength and consolation for the will, and the beginning of merit for the soul. This virtue broadens our knowledge of God and of divine things, of what God has revealed about His mysteries and His intimate life, of our elevation in Christ, of the indwelling of the Holy Spirit and of the whole spiritual organism in view of working for eternal life. Evangelical morality, which is immensely more perfect, more elevated, more extensive and more complete than the natural, is revealed to us by Jesus Christ in the Sermon on the Mount. It means a life lived as true children of God by adoption; it means imitation of Jesus Christ.

2. Faith is strength and consolation. It helps us consider the eternal reward: "Henceforth there is laid up for me the crown of righteousness" (2 Timothy 4:8). "For this slight momentary affliction is preparing for us an eternal weight of glory beyond all comparison" (2 Corinthians 4:17), wrote St. Paul. And elsewhere: "I consider that the sufferings of this present time are not worth comparing with the glory

that is to be revealed to us" (Romans 8:18). So then, one works, fights passions, burns with zeal, and performs the daily duties with joy. "...And this is the victory that overcomes the world, our faith" (1 John 5:4).

Faith is a font of merits, since every act of faith is already meritorious. It gives the right intention to our good deeds. Moreover, faith is proportionally much more meritorious when we are exposed to many dangers of losing it.

3. Faith is a gift of God, and therefore we must pray in order to increase it. Faith is our free adherence to Revelation, so it requires our effort. With prayer and practice, faith will become more firm, more active, more simple, more enlightened.

Intellectual pride causes many to disbelieve, or it makes their faith weak, ineffective, and irresolute in the face of temptations and enemies.

But faith can be perfected to the point of making us live by it. "My righteous one shall live by faith" (Hebrews 10:38).

Reflection—Is faith alive in me? Is it joyous? Firm? Active? Strong?

Resolution—I shall pray the Creed and the Act of Faith with great devotion.

Prayer—Lord, instill the gifts of wisdom and knowledge in me, along with an abundant outpouring of the Holy Spirit. May I live by faith! May I see Your hand in all guiding persons, things and events. Grant that I may reason, act and speak according to faith. May I witness to the following of the Gospel with prayer, words and deeds. May I be a true child of the Church—always humble, docile and fervent.

FAITH—III

"But blessed are your eyes, for they see, and your ears, for they hear. Truly, I say to you, many prophets and righteous men longed to see what you see, and did not see it, and to hear what you hear, and did not hear it.

"Hear then the parable of the sower."

—Matthew 13:16-18

1. According to St. Thomas, the study of religion is the most perfect, sublime, useful and joyous of all studies.

It is most *perfect* because it draws us closer to God and already gives us some share in the eternal vision of God. Therefore Scripture tells us: "Blessed is the man who meditates on wisdom" (Sirach 14:20).

The study of religion is most *sublime* because it renders man more like God, who does everything with wisdom. Wisdom is an infinite treasure for a person, and he who shares in it becomes a friend of God.

Studying religion is most *useful* because it assures us of eternal salvation. The desire for wisdom leads us to heaven.

The study of religion is most *joyous*, because talking about spiritual subjects never causes sadness. Nourishing ourselves on them never causes weariness, but brings happiness and joy.

2. However, it is necessary to have suitable spiritual dispositions:

a) The *right intention*, which is the glory of God and spiritual benefit for ourselves and others. St. Bernard wrote, "Some wish to learn only for the sake of knowledge, and this is vain curiosity. Others wish to learn in order to win esteem, and this is base vanity. Still others wish to learn in order to sell their knowledge for gain or for honors, and this is a sort of business. But there are those who wish to learn in order to help souls, and this is charity. Finally there are those who wish to learn in order to sanctify themselves, and this is holy prudence."

b) *A sincere love for truth.* Knowledge of religion is most trustworthy, because it comes from the Church, the infallible teacher. The objections of adversaries should not frighten us. Neither should we expound our own opinions; rather, we should adhere to the Church in everything.

c) *Humility.* Jesus says: "I thank you, Father, Lord of heaven and earth, that you have hidden these things from the wise and understanding and revealed them to babes" (Matthew 11:25).

The humble person prays. "If any of you lacks wisdom, let him ask God, who gives to all men generously and without reproaching..." (James 1:5).

Humility, then, generates charity, through which knowledge is used for edification.

d) *The desire to progress in the knowledge of God.* There are books and periodicals which at times arouse curiosity. Divine things, instead, are difficult to meditate in the beginning, but good will enables us to overcome all difficulties.

3. The Church places before us the examples of her great doctors: St. Gregory the Great, St Augustine, St. Thomas, St. Bonaventure, St. Albert the Great, St. Alphonsus, etc. They are true masters, models and protectors in this study of God and divine things, and it would be worthwhile to read

their lives and their works. Above all, it is very helpful to invoke them in difficulties.

Reflection—Do I love the study of the catechism and religion? Do I study it diligently? With humility? With the right intention? With love for the truth? With the desire to sanctify myself?

Resolution—Each day I shall do some spiritual reading.

Prayer—"In the beginning was the Word, and the Word was with God, and the Word was God.... All things were made through him, and without him was not anything made that was made.... The true light that enlightens every man was coming into the world. He was in the world, and the world was made through him, yet the world knew him not.... And the Word became flesh and dwelt among us.... Grace and truth came through Jesus Christ.... That whoever believes in him should not perish but have eternal life" (John 1:1, 3, 9, 10, 14, 17; 3:16).

FAITH—IV

"Take care, brethren, lest there be in any of you an evil, unbelieving heart, leading you to fall away from the living God. But exhort one another every day, as long as it is called 'today,' that none of you may be hardened by the deceitfulness of sin. For we share in Christ, if only we hold our first confidence firm to the end, while it is said,

'Today, when you hear his voice,
do not harden your hearts as in the rebellion.'"
—Hebrews 3:12-15

1. The dangers of losing one's faith, or at least of being influenced by errors regarding religious truths, are many.

Their sources may be conferences, or conversations, or the media. The irreligious and immoral press is a greater danger. A good part of the books, newspapers and publications of all kinds contain errors, attacks and heresies contrary to Catholicism. Often these are also found in novels, theatrical productions, etc. If one is not careful, little by little he will drink in this poison of unbelief or at least lose the purity of his faith. The result is that, weakened by doubts and insinuations, one will end up no longer able to defend himself.

Balmes, a profound and well-balanced man of talent, was obliged to read heretical books in order to refute them. He once said, "You know how deeply rooted I am in Catholic doctrine and ideas. Yet I am never able to use one of these books without then feeling the need to strengthen myself again by reading the *Bible, The Imitation of Christ,* or *Louis of Granata.* Now, what will become of so many careless young people who read anything and everything without precaution and without experience? Just the thought of it terrifies me."

2. St. Alphonsus de Liguori wrote: "Due to the wide distribution of leaflets and books against the Church, we see today a vast destruction of souls. If a spoken word, which 'flies' and is gone can spread like cancer and inflict a mortal wound, how much more damage can be expected from a bad book, which remains as a continual danger of perversion? But the natural law itself forbids the writing, printing, retaining, reading and spreading of such material. Parents, priests, civil leaders and educators are absolutely bound to a rigorous vigilance."

The Church has the duty of preserving and defending revealed doctrine.

3. The priceless gift of faith must be safeguarded through precautions and prayer. May the Divine Master be blessed for having given the gift of infallibility to the Church! No genius or school or book could be a surer guide than the Church, which is Jesus Christ Himself living and teaching through the centuries.

Reflection—The humble person distrusts himself. He makes himself a devout disciple of the Church, avoiding all dangerous literature, conversations and conferences.

How do I conduct myself?

Resolution—I shall consider faith which manifests itself in charity as the greatest treasure on earth.

Prayer—Act of Faith: O my God, I firmly believe that You are one God in three Divine Persons: Father, Son and Holy Spirit; I believe that Your Divine Son became man and died for our sins, and that He will come to judge the living and the dead. I believe these and all the truths which the holy Catholic Church teaches, because You have revealed them who can neither deceive nor be deceived.

HOPE—I

"Since then we have a great high priest who has passed through the heavens, Jesus, the Son of God, let us hold fast our confession. For we have not a high priest who is unable to sympathize with our weaknesses, but one who in every respect has been tempted as we are, yet without sinning. Let us then with confidence draw near to the

throne of grace, that we may receive mercy and find grace
to help in time of need."   —Hebrews 4:14-16

1. Hope is a theological virtue infused into our
soul by God. Through it we are inclined to desire
God as our Supreme Good and have the firm confidence of obtaining from Him paradise as well as the
means necessary to reach it. Faith shows us God as
the Supreme Good and eternal happiness.

Consequently there is born in us a supernatural
love for God along with a yearning to possess Him,
the desire to attain Him, through His grace and by
His promise, with good works.

The Christian desires God:
"I was glad when they said to me,
  'Let us go to the house of the Lord!'"
  (Psalm 122:1)

In order to achieve this goal graces are needed to
overcome temptations and acquire virtues and merits. One must also have the natural helps necessary
to work for eternal salvation and to remain in God's
service.

2. Hope is a great help and comfort in the work
of our sanctification. It unites us to God by detaching
us from the goods of the present life, such as the
esteem of men, temporal goods and pleasures.

Hope permits us to see these things now as
fleeting and worthless in themselves. They give little
consolation and vanish at death. The soul takes with
itself only the good or evil it has done. God alone is
the all; He is eternal, and inexhaustible joy.

Hope and trust are the necessary dispositions
to obtain graces. The divine promises are many:

"Truly, truly, I say to you, if you ask anything of the Father, he will give it to you in my name" (John 16:23). "Ask, and it will be given you; seek, and you will find; knock, and it will be opened to you" (Matthew 7:7).

Hope helps us to be generous in our activities. It inspires in us a lively desire for paradise, fervor in prayer, energy in work, and an assurance that God is with His faithful servants who trust in Him. "If God is for us, who is against us?" (Romans 8:31)

If Jesus Christ is with us, and we are really with Him, what harm can we fear from the demon and men? He who is sure of victory remains firm on the right road and in the apostolate.

3. Lord, I entrust myself entirely to You. I hope because You are merciful to the children who trust in You. I hope because You are all-powerful— therefore, You are able to grant all my desires. I hope because You promised us heaven and all the help necessary to attain it. Your word can never fail, even if men fail or the heavens pass away.

Reflection—Is my hope firm? Does it have a real effect on my sanctification? How do I pray?

Resolution—The Apostle wrote to Timothy: "As for the rich in this world, charge them not to be haughty, nor to set their hopes on uncertain riches but on God who richly furnishes us with everything to enjoy" (1 Timothy 6:17).

Prayer—You, O my God, assure me: "Who ever trusted in the Lord and was ever put to shame?" (Sirach 2:10) Was there ever anyone faithful in observing the commandments of God who was abandoned by Him? Or anyone who ever invoked Him and was forgotten? The Lord is kind and merciful and forgives sins. "He who did not spare his own Son but gave him up for us all, will he not also give us all things with him? Who shall bring any charges against God's elect? It is God who justifies; who is to condemn? Is it Christ Jesus, who died, yes, who was raised from the dead, who is at the right hand of God, who indeed intercedes for us?" (Romans 8:32-34)

HOPE—II

"Therefore gird up your minds, be sober, set your hope fully upon the grace that is coming to you at the revelation of Jesus Christ. As obedient children, do not be conformed to the passions of your former ignorance, but as he who called you is holy, be holy yourselves in all your conduct."   —1 Peter 1:13-15

1. One grows in hope through prayer and repeated acts of desire, trust and love for heavenly goods. Our Lord instills hope in the person who prays. Our cooperation is an indispensable condition for growth in every virtue. "We are God's fellow workers..." (1 Corinthians 3:9).

Just as God wants farmers to sow the seed, water and cultivate the crops, and then He gives life and growth, so too in the supernatural life.

Supernatural hope elevates natural hope. "...By the grace of God I am what I am, and his grace toward me was not in vain" (1 Corinthians 15:10). St. Paul exhorted, "Working together with him, then, we entreat you not to accept the grace of God in vain" (2 Corinthians 6:1). And to his disciple he wrote:

"Take your share of suffering as a good soldier of Christ Jesus" (2 Timothy 2:3).

In the same way, St. Peter spoke: "Be solicitous to make your call and election permanent, brothers; surely those who do so will never be lost" (2 Peter 1:10 NAB). To work, suffer, pray and struggle for heaven and for growth in virtue brings vigor and fervor to hope. Be firmly convinced, then, that the work of our sanctification depends entirely on God, but that it is also necessary to act as if everything depended on us alone. God never refuses His grace; so in practice we have to make every effort.

2. All of us must make acts of hope—at least from time to time, but especially in temptation and in danger of death.

There are two extremes we may encounter: presumption and despair. Presumption consists in expecting God to give us heaven and all the graces we need without any exertion on our part.... There are those who disregard the commandments, self-denial, prayer, effort and vigilance, and then believe that God will not permit them to be lost! Like Peter, they expose themselves needlessly to the occasions, unmindful of Christ's warning, "watch and pray" (Matthew 26:41); and they end up by falling.

Despair, discouragement and distress are the opposites of presumption, but these also cause one to abandon the means of salvation and sanctification.

Even St. Paul was convinced that by himself he did not have the strength to persevere. But full of trust he confided in the promise and grace of God: "Thanks be to God through Jesus Christ our Lord!" (Romans 7:25)

3. Let us raise our hearts and gaze heavenward, "so that we might see God in spirit in His heavenly glory" (cf. Alternate Opening Prayer, Liturgy of the Ascension); rather, let us "keep our hearts—even in the midst of the difficulties of this life—set on the place where true joys are" (cf. Easter Liturgy). This thought helps us to persevere and to pray for perseverance.

The attractions, intrigues and persecutions of the world are many. But St. Vincent used to say: "Even if the whole world were set against us to cause our ruin, it would not succeed if God did not will it. In Him lies all our hope."

God does everything for our good. Even physical and moral pain can be transformed into precious jewels for heaven.

Reflection—Do I nourish hope? Do I avoid both presumption and despair?

Resolution—With the trust of a child, I will abandon myself in the arms of God so that He may do with me whatever He pleases.

Prayer—Lord, I present to You my many miseries; have mercy on me. I am in danger of sin; save me. I am weighed down by sin; forgive me. My perseverance is uncertain; grant it to me through Your goodness. I fear difficulties in spiritual progress; give me Your support. I dread the thought of dying; at that moment come to my aid.

I hope against all hope. Oh! Grant me the grace to pray to You every day with trust. Mary, my mother, I shall always repeat to you: "Pray for me now, and at the hour of my death. Amen."

CHARITY—I

"And we have seen and testify that the Father has sent his Son as the Savior of the world. Whoever confesses that Jesus is the Son of God, God abides in him, and he in God. So we know and believe the love God has for us. God is love, and he who abides in love abides in God, and God abides in him."   —1 John 4:14-16

1. Faith sanctifies the mind, hope sanctifies the will, and charity sanctifies the sentiments.

Charity is a theological virtue infused by God into the soul. Through it we love God above everything else, since He is infinite goodness and our eternal happiness, and we love our neighbor for the love of God. Love of God and of our neighbor is really one virtue, that is, love of God in Himself or in His works. Love comes from God; it tends towards God; it unites us to God. God is infinitely great, powerful, good, true and beautiful. Therefore, He is infinitely lovable. He is one, but triune in Persons. He is the Father who from all eternity generates the Son and adopts us as children. He is the Son, equal to the Father, who through the Incarnation became our Brother and Redeemer. He is the Holy Spirit, the mutual love of the Father and Son, who infuses in us supernatural life. We love our neighbor because he is the image of God and because Jesus Christ loves everyone, because in him there is the hope of God, or at least it is desired for him. Simple souls love God much, and they gain great merit in this supernatural union of mind, will and heart with God.

2. The first and greatest commandment is: "...You shall love the Lord your God
   with all your heart,
   and with all your soul,
   and with all your mind,
   and with all your strength" (Mark 12:30).

St. Francis de Sales explains: "The love of God should prevail over all our loves and rule over all our passions. God requires this from us: that of all our loves His be the most *cordial*, dominating our entire heart; the most *affectionate*, filling our whole soul; the most *extensive*, engaging all our faculties; the most *noble*, captivating all our mind; the most *firm*, requiring all our strength and vigor." In a magnificent burst of love the saint concludes, "I am Yours, O Lord, only Yours. Yours is my soul, and I must live only for You; Yours is my will, and it must love only You; Yours is my heart, and it must strain toward You alone. I must love You as my first beginning, since I come from You. I must love You as my end and my rest, because I am destined for You. I must love You more than my being, for my being subsists because of You. I must love You more than myself, since I am totally in You and for You."

3. I understand, my Jesus, Divine Master, that I must love God as You taught me, as You loved the Father—that is, without limits and without reserve. I understand this when I ponder Your words at Gethsemane, "Father,...not my will, but yours, be done" (Luke 22:42).

This charity is commanded as our final goal: I live to unite myself to God. I must will it: I must apply myself to this always more. I must make every effort to attain it and to become more and more perfect. Then in heaven I will be able to possess charity completely and eternally.

Reflection—Did I understand well what the virtue of charity is? Do I desire to possess it? Do I constantly ask our Lord for it? Do I contemplate the charity of the heart of Jesus?

Resolution—I shall always aim for growth in charity, to the most perfect degree. I will love myself only for God, and love God for His own sake and for paradise.

Prayer—Act of Love: O my God, I love You above all things, with my whole heart and soul, because You are all good and worthy of all love. I love my neighbor as myself for the love of You. I forgive all who have injured me and I ask pardon of all whom I have injured.

CHARITY—II

"In this is love perfected with us, that we may have confidence for the day of judgment, because as he is so are we in this world. There is no fear in love, but perfect love casts out fear. For fear has to do with punishment, and he who fears is not perfected in love. We love, because he first loved us."   —1 John 4:17-19

1. Love of God is a gift from the Lord. It progresses with prayer and acts of charity. We receive the first infusion of love at our Baptism. Sin alone causes us to lose love.

Love of God *begins* with the avoidance of sin. This is *penitent* love. The person who detests offending God, avoids the occasions of sin, begs God's forgiveness in the Sacrament of Penance and prays in order to overcome temptations, already finds himself on the road to charity. The more he deplores his sins, the closer he draws to God.

Sentiments of humility and contrition are truly a beginning of love, and through divine goodness may soon be transformed into perfect love. St. Francis de Sales says, "Imperfect love desires God; it implores Him. Penitent love searches for Him and finds Him. Perfect love holds Him and clasps Him close."

Next is the love of *conformity,* which is present when we observe the commandments, fulfill the duties of our state in life and accept the trials of life. Grateful love leads us to consider how the Lord has pardoned our ingratitude and continues to shower graces upon us, still calling us to a high degree of sanctity. St. Peter is an encouraging example.

2. Charity progresses with the loves of complacency, benevolence and concupiscence.

The soul *delights* in all the divine attributes, in the infinite glory that God has in Himself. It is delighted that God is God and rejoices in His goodness. And if the soul is meditative, it progresses in this love: in silence and in quiet the devout soul advances.

The soul *loves* God, and desires that He receive that greater external glory which He still does not possess. We wish Him to receive the greatest glory first from us, and then from all other creatures. Hence, the Blessed Virgin sang: "My soul magnifies the Lord" (Luke 1:46). Moreover, we unite ourselves to the Church in desiring for Him that same eternal and infinite glory which the Divine Persons mutually exchange: "Glory to the Father and to the Son and to the Holy Spirit; as it was in the beginning, is now and will be forever. Amen."

The love of *concupiscence* is an ardent desire to be with God: to unite oneself on this earth to Jesus-Host in adoration, at Mass and in Communion, and in eternity to dwell always in the Heavenly Father's house.

3. Love becomes *perfect*, as much as this is possible on earth, by means of friendship. It includes reciprocity and mutual self-donation. From all eternity, God loves every heart which loves Him. He bestows His treasures and in exchange receives praise, adoration and acts of love from the soul. Continuously God speaks, attracts and comforts, while the soul seeks Him, listens to Him and loves Him in return. St. Francis de Sales said, "This friendship is not an ordinary friendship, but one of predilection with which we choose God so that we may love Him with a special love."

Reflection—Am I acquainted with the path or the ladder of charity? Have I begun to ascend it? Am I steadfast in climbing it? Do I aspire to everlasting charity?

Resolution—Each day I will try to ascend one step upward on this mystical ladder, which rests on earth but has its top in heaven.

Prayer—Lord, fill me with charity similar to the love You have for me. May I love You as You love me, O God of love. Yours is a perpetual love: "I have loved you with an everlasting love" (Jeremiah 31:3). It is a selfless love, because You love me only for my own good.

It is a generous love, for You give Yourself entirely to me.

It is an anticipated love, for You loved me even before I could understand Your love.

I understand Your heart: "I found delight in the sons of men" (Proverbs 8:31 NAB). May I love You with a constant, pure, generous and increasing love.

CHARITY—III

"Be imitators of God, as beloved children. And walk in love, as Christ loved us and gave himself up for us, a fragrant offering and sacrifice to God."

—Ephesians 5:1-2

1. The surpassing worth of the love of God is marvelously described by St. Paul: "If I speak in the tongues of men and of angels, but have not love, I am a noisy gong or a clanging cymbal. And if I have prophetic powers, and understand all mysteries and all knowledge, and if I have all faith, so as to remove mountains, but have not love, I am nothing. If I give away all I have, and if I deliver my body to be burned, but have not love, I gain nothing.

"Love is patient and kind; love is not jealous or boastful; it is not arrogant or rude. Love does not insist on its own way; it is not irritable or resentful; it does not rejoice at wrong, but rejoices in the right. Love bears all things, believes all things, hopes all things, endures all things.

"Love never ends.... So faith, hope, love abide, these three; but the greatest of these is love" (1 Corinthians 13:1-8, 13).

2. Charity is the virtue which sanctifies us the most. In fact, it unites a person entirely to God in mind, will and heart. It configures the soul with God, binds it to Him in an intimate friendship, and increases its ardor and strength. "Love is strong as death" (Song of Songs 8:6).

The *Imitation of Christ* describes the effects of charity: "It alleviates pain and lightens burdens, it carries the yoke without fatigue and sweetens every bitterness. Since charity is born of God, it lifts us up to Him, gives us wings to fly serenely on to always more perfect deeds and to a total gift of ourselves. It stimulates us on to great things, making us aim to what is more perfect. It is continually on the alert, does not complain of being overworked, and is not troubled by fear—but as a lively flame, it rises ever higher and, overcoming all obstacles, advances securely."

3. You, O Divine Master, have invited us to taste the sweetness of Your yoke and the lightness of Your burden. This yoke, this burden is love, and there is nothing sweeter, nothing more joyful, or nothing better in heaven or on earth. It is a foretaste of the eternal happiness of heaven: "To remain with Jesus is a sweet paradise." In fact, "If You, Lord, are present, all is joyous, but if You are absent all is burdensome."

Reflection—Do I know the science of charity? Do I desire charity? Do I practice it? Have I felt its effects?

Resolution—I will thirst to know the excelling knowledge of the love of Christ—to know its width and breadth, its height and depth.

Prayer—I shall contemplate Your heart, O Jesus. It is the theology, practice and prayer of living love. You manifested it to St. Margaret Mary Alacoque, encircled by a vivid light, surmounted by flames, bearing a cross, pierced by a lance and by a crown of sharpest thorns. The light is the knowledge of love; the cross, the proof of active love; the thorns, our venial sins; the lance, the symbol of serious sin. It is Way, Truth and Life. By loving the heart of Jesus, we can reach perfection quickly.

CHARITY—IV

"[Jesus] said to him, 'You shall love the Lord your God with all your heart, and with all your soul, and with all your mind.' This is the great and first commandment. And a second is like it, 'You shall love your neighbor as yourself.'"   —Matthew 22:37-39

1. Charity towards our neighbor is also a theological virtue. We love our neighbor for God's sake. To love our neighbor only for personal advantage, or for his own sake, would not be charity.

God is in our neighbor because He formed man according to His own image, giving him life as well as intelligence and free will.

Besides this, in our neighbor we see a child of God, a member of Jesus Christ and a co-heir of the heavenly kingdom. If our neighbor should not be in the state of grace we can help unite him to God by example, prayer and other means.

Loving our neighbor is one way of loving God. St. John writes: "We know that we have passed out of death into life, because we love the brethren....

Any one who hates his brother is a murderer"
(1 John 3:14, 15). "Beloved, let us love one another;
for love is of God, and he who loves is born of God
and knows God. He who does not love does not
know God; for God is love" (1 John 4:7-8). "If we love
one another, God abides in us and his love is
perfected in us" (1 John 4:12). "If any one says, 'I
love God,' and hates his brother, he is a liar" (1 John
4:20). "This commandment we have from him, that
he who loves God should love his brother also"
(1 John 4:21).

2. In the Gospel Jesus clearly and solemnly
declares that He considers done to Him whatever is
done for one's brother, even the least. "Truly, I say to
you, as you did it to one of the least of these my
brothers, you did it to me" (Matthew 25:40).

It is clear that Jesus Christ will not allow
Himself to be outdone in generosity. With all kinds
of graces, He rewards a hundredfold the least service
rendered Him in the person of one's neighbor.
St. John Eudes writes, "Look at your neighbor in
God, and at God in your neighbor. That is, look at
your neighbor as being loved with God's goodness.
Look at him as one who shares in the life of God, as
created to return to God, to be placed in God's bosom
to glorify Him either through mercy or justice."

This is very consoling for those who care for the
sick, who give alms, or who help a neighbor spiritually. It is even more so for those who consecrate their
entire lives to works of the apostolate and of charity.
These serve Jesus in the person of their neighbor at
every instant. In return, Christ adorns their souls
with virtue and sanctifies them.

3. St. Paul writes: "I therefore, a prisoner for the Lord, beg you to lead a life worthy of the calling to which you have been called, with all lowliness and meekness, with patience, forbearing one another in love, eager to maintain the unity of the Spirit in the bond of peace. There is one body and one Spirit, just as you were called to the one hope that belongs to your call,...one God and Father of us all, who is above all and through all and in all" (Ephesians 4:1-4, 6). "Rather, speaking the truth in love, we are to grow up in every way into him who is the head, into Christ" (Ephesians 4:15).

Reflection—Have I penetrated well the motives for loving my neighbor? Is my charity supernatural? Do I think about the eternal salvation of my neighbor?

Resolution—I shall be charitable with my neighbor in mind and heart, word and deed.

Prayer—I reflect on and pray with the words of St. Paul: "So if there is any encouragement in Christ, any incentive of love,...complete my joy by being of the same mind, having the same love, being in full accord and of one mind. Do nothing from selfishness or conceit, but in humility count others better than yourselves. Let each of you look not only to his own interests, but also to the interests of others" (Philippians 2:1-4).

CHARITY—V

"Let love be generous; hate what is evil, hold fast to what is good; love one another with brotherly affection; outdo one another in showing honor. Never flag in zeal, be aglow with the Spirit, serve the Lord. Rejoice in your hope, be patient in tribulation, be constant in prayer."

—Romans 12:9-12

1. Perfect charity is *supernatural* because it makes us see Jesus Christ in our neighbor. It is *universal*, since it makes no distinction or classification of persons; *generous*, because it has no limits except impossibility; and *active*, because it reveals itself above all in deeds.

In the first place, love towards our neighbor makes us avoid evil. Charity in *thought* avoids rash judgment; it does not condemn anyone at first sight, or for petty reasons, without considering his intentions well. It drives away ill-founded suspicions. With regard to the *sentiments*, charity avoids antipathies and unhealthy partialities, which if consented to are often true faults against charity. Charity excludes rivalry, hatred and envy, which drive hearts apart and often cause words and actions which displease the Lord and destroy peace. In *words* charity avoids quarrels and haughty and proud disputes in which everyone wants the triumph of his own ideas and the humiliation of his neighbor. These result in false accusations, discord and unjust criticism, sources of friction and dissention in the great Christian family. However, charity avoids harsh, mocking and scornful words which generate or stimulate animosities.

2. Our Savior used very strong words about those who give scandal: "Whoever causes one of these little ones who believe in me to sin, it would be better for him to have a great millstone fastened

round his neck and to be drowned in the depth of the sea" (Matthew 18:6). Scandal may be given through conversations contrary to faith or to other virtues, by songs, by omissions or by actions which are an occasion of spiritual harm to souls. St. Paul wants us to avoid even those words and actions which, although indifferent in themselves, may become an incentive to evil because of the ignorance or weakness of one's neighbor. He wants the more instructed to take their neighbor's scruples into account. "Do not let your knowledge destroy him for whom Christ died" (cf. Romans 14:15).

3. We must avoid revenge in words and deeds. "If you forgive men their trespasses, your heavenly Father also will forgive you; but if you do not forgive men their trespasses, neither will your Father forgive your trespasses" (Matthew 6:14-15). In fact, we pray to Him thus:

"...forgive us our trespasses
as we forgive those who trespass against us"
    (cf. Matthew 6:12).

Bossuet says, "The first gift we must offer God is a heart free from all coldness and all hostility towards one's neighbor."

St. Paul says explicitly, "Do not let the sun go down on your anger" (Ephesians 4:26).

A saint advises: Do not reason that your adversary is more to blame than you, and should therefore apologize first. Jesus Christ, instead, was the first to pardon and help His crucifiers by crying out in a loud voice, "Father, forgive them; for they know not what they do" (Luke 23:34).

Reflection—Do I know the sins against charity well? Do I detest them? Do I avoid thoughts, sentiments, words and actions opposed to this virtue?

Resolution—I shall be on the alert, knowing that faults against charity pierce the heart of our neighbor and go on to wound the heart of Jesus.

Prayer—My God, You are charity, and all that promotes charity pleases You and establishes Your presence within us. All that lacerates and offends charity removes Your presence from us. Grant me the grace to love tenderly. May I think well of everyone; may I judge everyone well; may I speak well of everyone; may I do good to all. I must imitate You in everything, O Lord, but especially in love.

CHARITY—VI

"I say to you, Love your enemies and pray for those who persecute you, so that you may be sons of your Father who is in heaven; for he makes his sun rise on the evil and on the good, and sends rain on the just and on the unjust."
—Matthew 5:44-45

1. Jesus tells us: "This is my commandment, that you love one another as I have loved you" (John 15:12). Bossuet comments, "It is a new commandment, because He wants us to love our neighbor as *He loved us*: namely, with a most perfect love."

First, we must bear with our neighbor in spite of his defects. How many defects did Christ have to bear with in His own Apostles! How many defects do we have that weigh heavily on others!

Let us love, because God first loved us, even while we were still His enemies—"While we were yet helpless, Christ died for the ungodly" (Romans 5:6). Jesus anticipated the Samaritan woman, the adulteress, the thief. These are divine courtesies which we have to imitate by seeking out our brothers and sisters, the poor, sinners, children and vocations.

Moreover, charity is to be *compassionate*. These words of Christ should penetrate the heart of every Christian: "I have compassion on the crowd" (Mark 8:2). Jesus fed the hungry; He instituted the sacraments, which are channels of grace; He dealt most tenderly with children; He healed the sick. If possible, let us give alms or a little time, comfort, courtesy, advice or spiritual aid.

2. Let ours be *generous* charity, since Jesus "loved me and gave himself for me" (Galatians 2:20). We will serve our neighbors even at the cost of painful sacrifices, even if their wounds are repulsive or if those for whom we care are almost rebellious. Let us do so with *cordiality:* sometimes the way we perform an act means more than what is actually done; with *intelligence:* to put someone in the condition of earning his bread means more than giving him bread itself; with the *spirit of apostles,* desiring to reach the soul through the body, always remembering that, "whoever brings back a sinner from the error of his way will save his soul from death and will cover a multitude of sins" (James 5:20).

3. *Immolative* charity. Since Jesus gave His life for us, we, too, must give our life for our neighbor.

Apostolic lay persons, priests and sisters often offer their lives hour by hour, drop by drop, working tirelessly for souls. By prayer, sermons, study and various works, they put St. Paul's program into action: "I will most gladly spend and be spent for your souls. If I love you the more, am I to be loved the less?" (2 Corinthians 12:15)

Some have reached the point of taking the *vow of servitude* to souls, obliging themselves to consider souls as their superiors, giving them the right to demand obedience to their every desire.

Reflection—Do I have the positive program of Christian charity well impressed on my mind? How much of it have I already put into effect? Do I pray to advance along this divine path, following Jesus who precedes me?

Resolution—I will reflect on the life of Jesus. His actions are precepts. As He did, I must also do.

Prayer—Finally, O my Divine Master, I must make the sentiments of Your heart my own: "Love your enemies, do good to those who hate you, bless those who curse you, pray for those who abuse you" (Luke 6:27-28). Your grace alone can place these sentiments in my heart. Sacred Heart of Jesus, I place my trust in You.

PRUDENCE—I

"The tendency of the flesh is toward death but that of the spirit toward life and peace. The flesh in its tendency is at enmity with God; it is not subject to God's law. Indeed, it cannot be; those who are in the flesh cannot please God."   —Romans 8:6-8 (NAB)

1. Prudence is a moral and supernatural virtue which inclines the mind to choose the best means to assure eternal salvation and to do good works.

There are prudent industrialists, businessmen, farmers, students and workers. To be successful these persons organize and direct their earthly interests, displaying their human prudence.

There is the prudence of those who are sensual, ambitious and miserly. This is prudence of the flesh, the enemy of God, which leads to death.

Christian prudence, instead, once it knows the eternal destiny of man, directs everything to the conquest of heaven. All human duties, thoughts, intentions and sentiments, though they may branch out in many directions, have only one purpose—our attainment of heaven. "True and perfect prudence is that which advises, judges, and pushes straight ahead towards the ultimate goal of life," says St. Thomas.

2. The parable of the ten virgins helps us better to understand the meaning of prudence.

"The kingdom of heaven shall be compared to ten maidens who took their lamps and went to meet the bridegroom. Five of them were foolish, and five were wise. For when the foolish took their lamps, they took no oil with them; but the wise took flasks of oil with their lamps. As the bridegroom was delayed, they all slumbered and slept. But at midnight there was a cry, 'Behold, the bridegroom! Come out to meet him.' Then all those maidens rose and trimmed their lamps. And the foolish said to the wise, 'Give us some of your oil, for our lamps are going out.' But the wise replied, 'Perhaps there will not be enough for us and for you; go rather to the dealers and buy for yourselves.' And while they went to buy, the bridegroom came, and those who were ready went in with him to the marriage feast; and the door was shut. Afterward the other maidens came also, saying, 'Lord, lord, open to us.' But he replied, 'Truly, I say to you, I do not know you.' Watch therefore, for you know neither the day nor the hour'' (Matthew 25:1-13).

3. Reason enlightened by faith shows us the reward. Once this is well rooted, the means are arranged. "For the joy that was set before him [he] endured the cross..." (Hebrews 12:2). Thus one directs his whole life, as well as each daily action and word, towards eternal happiness.

Reflection—Am I well enlightened, penetrated by supernatural principles? Do I believe firmly in the Last Things—death, judgment, hell and heaven? Do I direct my actions toward eternity?

Resolution—I need light; I shall always ask it of God. It is that light which must enlighten my steps and lead me to eternal life.

Prayer—Lord, thousands of shadows, snares and human weaknesses make salvation a difficult task for me. But I trust in You! He who trusts in the Lord will rise in the Lord. I shall turn to the fonts of life and grace; these You have given to us in the holy sacraments. May I always understand better the good I can find in the sacrament of Penance, in Communion, in the Mass and in Eucharistic Adoration. It is there that I find You always present. Each day I can talk to You; I can listen to Your holy, adorable words, and receive inexpressible joy and comfort. With You I am secure; I shall ascend my little Calvary and reach heaven.

PRUDENCE—II

"Look carefully then how you walk, not as unwise men but as wise, making the most of the time, because the days are evil. Therefore do not be foolish, but understand what the will of the Lord is."   —Ephesians 5:15-17

1. Prudence examines with maturity, resolves with wisdom and works with fidelity.

In the first place prudence examines well the final purpose. Many are mistaken regarding this essential point. Why was I created? Why do I exist? To answer this serious question a mature examination is necessary.

We must reflect on our past, because experience is the teacher of life. We can think of the difficulties encountered, the failures and the victories. History, too, is an aid, since it helps us to know the good or evil done by those who preceded us, as well as what helps or obstacles we ourselves encountered.

Reflection on present circumstances and the foreseeable future is also important. It is always prudent to seek counsel. Sometimes, very wise persons who love us, as well as persons young in age, with less education or a lower position, are able to enlighten us about dangers. They can even reveal an aspect we had not considered before and give us useful advice. In cases of important decisions, we must ask this enlightenment above all from God, with the prayer "Come, Holy Spirit" or with other prayers.

2. We must resolve wisely by choosing means which lead more securely toward the final purpose of life. To this end we must carefully remove prejudices, passions and impressions which disturb our judgment. What will this serve me for eternity? What would I wish to have done when I find myself at the point of death or at the judgment? Not wanting to deceive himself, the Christian examines all these things with deep discernment; then he concludes decisively, without excessive hesitation.

We can always trust in God when we have used all the means which He has prepared for us. Even if we make mistakes materially, God's help and reward will not be lacking. He will be with us to comfort us; He will be with us to reward at least our effort of good will.

3. Faithful fulfillment: In spite of all the calculations and good will, we always need humility. It is also necessary to take the means which are more powerful and effective, to avoid giving up in the face of some defeat. Caution is needed: to open one's eyes, to notice the qualities of persons, to keep watch over the course of internal and external events. We must use all precautions: "Look carefully then how you walk" (Ephesians 5:15). The enemy prepares difficulties and evil designs which are all the more crafty in proportion to the beauty and holiness of the resolutions. By being alert, one does not fall victim to sudden or unexpected surprises, is not perturbed, and has the strength to rise and start over again. With

the help of divine grace, there is the strength to bring to a successful conclusion the work of personal sanctification as well as all the good initiatives of apostolate and of good works.

Reflection—How much consideration do I give before making a decision? How do I make resolutions? How do I carry them out?

Resolution—Be prudent in mind, prudent in sentiments, prudent in actions.

Prayer—I will meditate on the words of St. James in regard to true wisdom or prudence:

"The wisdom from above is first pure, then peaceable, gentle, open to reason, full of mercy and good fruits, without uncertainty or insincerity" (James 3:17).

This wisdom is modest in mind and heart and tranquil, since it conserves the necessary calm. It is humble because it is agreeable and yet persuasive, since it follows sound reasoning. It is full of mercy for those who have fallen and always obtains good results. It is not partial, nor is it hypocritical or deceitful.

JUSTICE

"You are righteous and rule all things righteously,
deeming it alien to your power
to condemn him who does not deserve to be punished.
For your strength is the source of righteousness,
and your sovereignty over all causes you to spare all....
Through such works you have taught your people
that the righteous man must be kind,
and you have filled your sons with good hope,
because you give repentance for sins."

—Wisdom 12:15, 16, 19

1. Justice is a moral and supernatural virtue which inclines the will to give to everyone his due.

Charity gives to one's neighbor even what is not strictly due. Bossuet says, "When I talk about justice, I am also talking about the sacred bond of human society, the necessary brake of license.... When justice rules, we find faith in treaties, honesty in affairs and order in politics. The earth is at peace. Even heaven, so to speak, gladly sends its light and gently influences us."

Justice is *general* if we refer to society at large or to the societies in which we live. It is *particular* if we refer to rights and duties of citizens towards each other. General justice obliges us to carry our share of the burden of society in recompense for the many benefits we receive from it. According to the times and circumstances, we owe to society: services, taxes, part of our own goods and even some of our liberty. Particular justice regulates the rights and duties among citizens as regards material goods, reputation, liberty and the goods of body and soul.

2. Justice is the beginning of order and peace in the lives of individuals, as well as in society as a whole. If justice reigns, business is honest, fraud is repressed, the helpless and humble are defended, citizens obey, and rulers justly distribute the burdens and profits of life in society.

If, moreover, all the duties of justice are fulfilled for God, according to the infusion of grace, they will have supernatural value and will reap reward in eternal life. Where there is fear of God, there is also a thoughtful respect for all that belongs to our neighbor. Hence the soldier, doctor, teacher, judge and citizen who are good Christians will also be the most faithful in their respective duties. They will be most exemplary and worthy of trust in society. Thus, in his individual, social and political life, the Christian fulfills his duties with a special sense of responsibility and always in view of God and eternity. By this he makes great progress in spiritual life and in sanctity.

3. I will respect the right of ownership, avoiding petty thefts, damage, deceit and unlawful speculations. I shall refrain from contracting exaggerated debts and shall be prompt in paying those contracted. I shall make reparation for any harm I have caused others. I shall use with care whatever belongs to others and shall promptly return anything borrowed. In sacred matters and in almsgiving I shall be especially conscientious. I shall respect the reputation of others, avoiding any calumny, murmuring, slander, or violation of secrets. If I have fallen short in something, I shall try to make speedy reparation.

Reflection—Am I well informed in regard to these obligations of justice? In my office as a professional, a parent, or a business person, am I without blame? Do I examine myself, confess my failures and improve myself in this most delicate virtue?

Resolution—In my examination I shall pause at the point which concerns me most.

Prayer—O Lord, Zacchaeus, enlightened by grace, declared, "Behold, Lord, the half of my goods I give to the poor; and if I have defrauded any one of anything, I restore it fourfold" (Luke 19:8). You replied, "Today salvation has come to this house" (Luke 19:9). Grant that I may always act with justice, for Your sake and for the reward reserved for the just. "The righteous live forever, and their reward is with the Lord" (Wisdom 5:15).

FORTITUDE

"Finally, be strong in the Lord and in the strength of his might. Put on the whole armor of God, that you may be able to stand against the wiles of the devil. For we are not contending against flesh and blood, but against the principalities, against the powers, against the world rulers of this present darkness, against the spiritual hosts of wickedness in the heavenly places. Therefore take the whole armor of God, that you may be able to withstand in the evil day, and having done all, to stand."—Ephesians 6:10-13

1. Fortitude is a moral and supernatural virtue which makes the soul generous and intrepid in its work for heaven in spite of any difficulty, fear or even death itself. The staunch heart knows how to take these on and endure them. There are obstacles, temptations and fears involved in following the path of virtue and fulfilling the duties of any state of life. One must face them with courage. Fortitude leads us to make resolutions without any fear, to act with the necessary strength, and to continue to the end. He who wills to become a saint does so! But only he who really wills it!

There is a complexity of sufferings to be borne: sickness, interior battles, repugnance, derision, calumny. Many times these things can be more painful than fatigue, says St. Thomas. A long illness, especially if painful, an insult, or a sneer from someone are often harder to bear than fatigue.

2. Jesus Christ is an example of fortitude in difficult undertakings. With courage He began His public ministry, which would cost Him endless toil and contradiction. He went to Jerusalem, even though He foresaw suffering and humiliation. In His Passion, He bore internal and external sufferings, most numerous and unspeakable, with unalterable patience and serenity.

Much merit is gained and much good is done when one has the courage to undertake great things for the Lord, the Church, souls, society and the poor. Then, time, skill, and money are used in worthwhile enterprises of art, good works and education. It is not necessary to be rich; Divine Providence will provide the means. Stinginess, instead, is a sign of a narrow and egoistic soul and careless squandering is a sign of imbalance and disorder.

A strong, patient person earns countless merits. He remains calm in the midst of pain, bending neither to the right nor to the left. He continues on his way towards heaven. Every Christian has his share of the cross—the internal and external sufferings which, in general, are caused by daily life.

3. Deliver me, O Lord, from useless fears and instill in me the precious gift of fortitude. It is true that there are fatigue and dangers, but the only true evil is sin. From all other evils one can derive a wealth of merits and eternal glory. There are criticism and ridicule, but none of these take anything away from what we have or what we are before God. To be governed by human respect is cowardice. Often one who outwardly sneers at good people inwardly admires and envies them.

At times one may offend his friends by living a righteous life. However, it would be far more serious to displease God by neglecting one's duty. St. Paul says that if he had pleased men, he would not have been the servant of Christ. God alone is our judge, and His judgment is what really counts.

Reflection—Am I convinced of these truths? Am I generous? Do I endure life's trials? Do I look at my exemplar, Jesus Crucified?

Resolution—I shall keep this thought in mind: God sees me! It is not he who praises himself who is worthy of praise, but he who has the approval of God.

Prayer—Lord, I am feeble and weak. Come to me with the fullness of Your grace. The occasions of great merit are few, and should one arise, I might not be able to accept it. I want to exert my courage and patience in the many tiny occasions which are part of life. The constant practice of little acts of virtue very often demands the same or even greater heroism than great deeds. Since I am unable to accomplish great things, I shall offer these small flowers to You with love and a spirit of humility. Accept them, O my Divine Master, for Your glory!

TEMPERANCE

"I say, walk by the Spirit, and do not gratify the desires of the flesh. For the desires of the flesh are against the Spirit, and the desires of the Spirit are against the flesh; for these are opposed to each other, to prevent you from doing what you would."   —Galatians 5:16-17

1. Temperance is the virtue which moderates the soul. It mortifies the passions, submitting them to reason.

St. Augustine describes temperance well. "The temperate man has a certain rule governing the things of this life...so that he is a slave to none of them. He does not desire anything for mere satisfaction or pleasure, but always makes use of everything at the proper time with simplicity."

Temperance moderates all the passions and produces many virtues in our hearts.

2. The fruits of temperance are many: *Continence* curbs the emotions of sensuality as well as the immoderate desire for food and drink. It is the strength of souls who impose an orderly way of life on themselves and faithfully practice it. *Meekness* curbs impulsive anger so that a person does not become angry except when and in the measure which is required to avoid sin and to do good. *Mildness* mitigates punishment, leads to proper compassion and fosters pardon. *Humility* curbs the immoderate desire for honor, praise and pomp. It also moderates false and excessive self-esteem. *Modesty* puts in order the movements of the body, and moderates speech and actions. It reduces to just limits any tendencies toward vanity in regard to dress, food and adornment. *Studiousness* regulates the desire for knowledge, so that this does not develop into a passion; it curbs vain curiosity and the desire for useless knowledge. *L'eutrapelia* or politeness requires moderation in games, amusements and entertainment. At times it is necessary to be mortified even in things which are lawful or indifferent in themselves in order to avoid following only pleasures.

3. O Jesus Master, perfect model of every virtue, deliver me from the overindulgence of my passions. May the light of Your examples always shine brightly before my eyes. Help me with Your grace.

I confess that I am weak and that many times I have been intemperate in regard to gluttony, anger, greed, curiosity, and excessive rest. Jesus Master, Way, Truth and Life, have pity on me.

Reflection—Temperance is a cardinal virtue. Do I understand this? Am I among those who have no rule in life and who moment by moment do what pleases them the most? Good resolutions are useful, but to put them into practice prayer is necessary above all.

Resolution—I will restore within myself the ordered reign of will and faith, overthrown by sin.

Prayer—Lord, help me with Your divine mercy, so that I may live as a person and a Christian. Grant that I may overcome weakness and anger and practice true meekness. May I conquer gluttony and practice mortification. May I control pride and practice holy humility. May I overcome vanity and practice Christian modesty. May I overcome vain curiosity and love true wisdom. May I control my speech and all intemperate actions, and live according to a rule established with the advice of a spiritual director.

HUMILITY—I

"Such is the confidence that we have through Christ toward God. Not that we are sufficient of ourselves to claim anything as coming from us; our sufficiency is from God."   —2 Corinthians 3:4-5

1. Humility is the virtue which inclines us to know and reflect upon ourselves and wish to be taken at our true value.

Humility is truth. Humility of mind is the profound conviction that as *created* beings we have nothing of our own. In fact, in the supernatural order, not a single thing is ours, since we have received everything which was not even required by our created nature. Then, as *sinners*, we have offended God, and nothing—not even punishment, humiliations or sorrow—could suffice to repay the debt thus contracted with Divine Justice.

We are *called to sanctity*, but by ourselves we can do nothing. Cooperation with grace is so uncertain that without God's help we cannot even hope for sanctity. St. Thomas says that two things can be considered in man: what belongs to God and what belongs to man. What is a defect belongs to man, while everything pertaining to perfection and salvation belongs to God.

2. Humility is *justice*. If in the order of nature and of grace we have nothing, then to God alone go honor, gratitude and adoration. I would commit an injustice if I would aim for praise; I would be robbing God of the glory which belongs to Him alone. If I am a sinner, I have offended God to such an extent—have committed such acts of rashness and foolishness—that not even all the insults I may receive from men can ever compare with the offense I have committed against God. No matter how foolish, imprudent and guilty I may be judged, no one can ever fully weigh all the enormity of my foolishness and guilt.

Sin contains a certain infinity of malice. If God alone gives good thoughts, good resolutions, and the fulfillment of them, then I depend entirely upon Him. It is He who acts. On the other hand, I should always remain humbly in the Lord's presence, pleading that He continue to bestow His mercy. Just as I would not be able to subsist without an almost continual creation in the natural order, so I would not be able to persevere in doing good without a most particular action of grace. Neither would I be able to reach eternal salvation, even if I were already as perfect as St. Aloysius. "...Apart from me you can do nothing" (John 15:5).

3. Humility is order. Everyone in his place! God is God and I am nothing. Therefore, it follows that I must conduct myself as nothing. I should live in total submission to whatever God disposes. I am like a criminal who escaped from prison, not because he was unseen, but because he received a pardon. I am like a newly-grafted shoot which receives all its life-giving sap from the vine—Christ—or like a very fragile reed, easily bent by the wind. I am so limited in intelligence. God instead is the truth. I am so full of unruly passions, while God is sanctity itself. I am so inconstant, while God is unchangeable. I live at the edge of the grave, while God is eternal. "What have you that you did not receive?" (1 Corinthians 4:7)

What shall I say on judgment day—I, proud, dust and ashes?

Reflection—Am I really convinced that humility is rooted in fundamental truths? What is the truth regarding our actual being and the Infinite Being, God? Do I consider humility as justice towards God? As the order by which I consider God precisely for what He is and put myself in the place which is due to me?

Resolution—I will reflect that in order to have faith, to be just and to have respect for order, I must be interiorly humble, first of all in my thoughts.

Prayer—Jesus Master, meek and humble of heart, make my heart like Yours.

When the Virgin Mary was acknowledged and greeted as Mother of God, she gave praise to God in these words: "My soul magnifies the Lord.... He who is mighty has done great things for me, and holy is his name" (Luke 1:49). St. Paul writes: "By the grace given to me I bid every one among you not to think of himself more highly than he ought to think, but to think with sober judgment, each according to the measure of faith which God has assigned him" (Romans 12:3).

HUMILITY—II

"Have this mind among yourselves, which was in Christ Jesus, who, though he was in the form of God, did not count equality with God a thing to be grasped, but emptied himself, taking the form of a servant, being born in the likeness of men. And being found in human form he humbled himself and became obedient unto death, even death on a cross."   —Philippians 2:5-8

1. We understand the great worth of the virtue of humility first of all from the fact that Jesus, the infallible Teacher, esteemed and practiced it. The Son of God, equal to the Father in glory and power, became man and humbled Himself at every moment of His life, especially during His passion and in the Holy Eucharist. Thus His Father exalted Him above every name, since He had touched the very depths of humiliation.

At Bethlehem, we contemplate Him as a poor, weak infant, lying on a few pieces of straw in a manger. There was no room for Him among men, so He was compelled to be born in a cave which served as a shelter for animals.

At the end of His earthly life, ungrateful mankind boldly shouted: "Away with him, away with him, crucify him!" (John 19:15)

Remaining silent, as if unable to defend Himself, He endured all this from His creatures to whom He had brought salvation.

As a small child He fled into Egypt. On His return He concealed Himself in a very poor house in a town that everyone despised, and led a hidden life there for thirty years. He obeyed as if He were unable to guide Himself, worked as a common laborer and served His Mother and Joseph even in insignificant matters. No wonder Bossuet exclaims, "Come, O proud man, and die before such a spectacle."

2. In His public life, Jesus preached, performed miracles and declared Himself to be the Son of God. But all of this was only for God's glory, done in a spirit of obedience, for the salvation of mankind.

He addressed Himself especially to the poor and He lived on charity. For His friends and apostles He chose a few fishermen and a tax collector. He spoke simply and avoided popularity, seeking only His Father's glory. He did not have even a stone to call His own. Often He forbade His miracles to be publicized and on various occasions He talked about His passion. He closed His life in a series of humiliations which are a mystery to us.

Let us contemplate Him at Gethsemane, or bent beneath the blows of scourges, or during the mockery of the crowning with thorns.

He was sold by an apostle, denied by the very one He had chosen as the foundation of the Church, and abandoned by all. He was condemned by the religious, military, and political courts. He was almost submerged in a sea of accusations, wounded in His dignity as man, as king and as judge.

The criminal Barabbas was preferred to Him and Jesus was condemned to the cross. Bowed down beneath the heavy weight of the instrument of torture, He walked to Calvary, where He was stripped of His garments and crucified. He was in agony for three hours and died between two thieves. And yet He always remained silent, suffering and praying for those who struck Him, giving mankind the supreme proof of His love.

3. St. Vincent de Paul says, "The life of our Lord was like a continual act of esteem and affection for contempt. His heart was so full of it that if an autopsy had been made (as was done on a particular saint) it would certainly have been found that holy humility was deeply carved in the adorable heart of Jesus. And without risk of exaggeration, one can affirm that it was carved there in preference to all other virtues."

Reflection—Have I pondered deeply the mystery of the humiliations of Jesus? Do I love humility? Do I yearn for humiliations as Jesus did?

Resolution—By contemplating Jesus, my love and my model, I will cherish embarrassment, blame and calumny.

Prayer—O my Savior, how much You loved this virtue! Why did You submit to this extreme abasement? Only because You understood well the excellence of humiliation and the malice of the opposite sin. Pride not only aggravates other sins, but also corrupts actions which in themselves would not be sinful, even those very actions which are good or holy. O Jesus, forgive my vanity, my pride, my inconstancy. Grant me time to repent and correct myself.

HUMILITY—III

"Jesus came from Galilee to the Jordan to John, to be baptized by him. John would have prevented him, saying, 'I need to be baptized by you, and do you come to me?' But Jesus answered him, 'Let it be so now; for thus it is fitting for us to fulfill all righteousness.'"   —Matthew 3:13-15

1. The great worth of the virtue of humility can also be deduced from its fruits. It is the key to divine treasures. The Lord necessarily aims at His own glory in all His works. Therefore He will give His favors to the one who recognizes them as His gifts, who is grateful to Him and gives Him glory. He cannot do otherwise: "My glory I give to no other..." (Isaiah 42:8). "God opposes the proud, but gives grace to the humble" (James 4:6). Proud people are like mountains. The waters of divine grace do not rest on them and they remain arid. The humble are like valleys in which the waters are gathered. "Every

valley shall be filled and every mountain and hill shall be brought low" (Luke 3:5). Humility, therefore, inclines the beneficent goodness of the divine heart to give, and prepares hearts of men to receive.

The goodness of God is diffusive, but the proud person stops and impedes this diffusion. The humble person allows this goodness to expand and enriches himself with it.

2. Humility is the negative foundation and nourishes every virtue. The theological and cardinal virtues are infused by the Holy Spirit, but this Spirit does not dwell in a heart that is proud and puffed up with knowledge or power. Instead, He communicates Himself to the simple. And so it is that our Lord reveals His wisdom to the little ones who have a sincere, profound spirit of *faith*. The humble person hopes in God, not in himself, and his hope is strengthened and becomes fruitful.

Charity is opposed to egoism, which is self-love, pride and haughtiness. Humility makes a man *prudent* and distrustful of himself. The proud person exaggerates his own rights and forgets his neighbor's, while the humble person practices justice. Conscious of his weakness, the humble person finds his *strength* in God. Humility is also a good guardian of *temperance* and *chastity*.

3. The humble person enjoys great peace as well as frequent and intimate communication with the Lord, and He willingly remains where Providence has placed him.

Perhaps he appears little before men, but the eyes of the Lord turn to him with satisfaction and he earns great merit for heaven. St. Augustine tells us, "Do you wish to be exalted? Begin by humbling yourself. Are you thinking of constructing a very high building? First lay the foundation of humility."

Reflection—Do I value humility greatly? Do I desire it? Do I seek it? Do I ask it of God?

Resolution—In my everyday life I shall practice humility towards God, my neighbor and myself.

Prayer—O Lord, let me understand Your words: "When you are invited by anyone to a marriage feast, do not sit down in a place of honor, lest a more eminent man than you be invited by him; and he who invited you both will come and say to you, 'Give place to this man,' and then you will begin with shame to take the lowest place. But when you are invited, go and sit in the lowest place, so that when your host comes he may say to you, 'Friend, go up higher'; then you will be honored in the presence of all" (Luke 14:8-10).

The lowest place belongs to me, because I am a great sinner.

HUMILITY—IV

"Let the greatest among you become as the youngest, and the leader as one who serves."   —Luke 22:26

1. Interior humility concerns the *mind* and *heart*. St. Bernard says that humility is the truest concept of oneself, which leads a person to *despise* himself. This does not mean that he despises God's gifts. Rather, these gifts lead him to adore, love and praise God, who gave them to him. But, the person despises himself inasmuch as he is a mere "noth-

ing," a sinner, incapable of anything in the supernatural realm. "...Apart from me you can do nothing" (John 15:5), neither little, nor much, but nothing at all, says St. Augustine, and this is a doctrine of faith.

Humility of heart leads us to love our nothingness, baseness and inability. The humble person does not hold himself in esteem. He is happy that God is God, that He is the Beginning, the End, the Ruler, the Judge, the supreme and highest Good.

A humble person is always inclined to praise and adore God—to God alone all praise and glory. He is always most grateful and thankful to the Lord and will readily recognize his sins. He is the first to admit his defects. A humble person is always willing to ask God for help. He trusts not so much in his own ability but implores the Lord. He spends much time in prayer, to which he gives the greatest importance.

2. The mere awareness of our misery is not sufficient, although it is the truth. We must also *love* our nothingness. If a sin has been committed, it most certainly should be detested. At the same time, however, we ought to love the lowliness to which this sin has reduced us. Rejoice in the fact that God will be praised for all eternity, not only because He forgave us original sin, but also because He pardoned our actual sins. Because of this mercy, He will be glorified for all eternity. Our misery will exalt the divine goodness.

A humble person inwardly enjoys being considered good-for-nothing, a sinner and imperfect; therefore, he also enjoys being despised, criticized and overlooked. He loves to be forgotten and considered as nothing.

When a humble person sees that God uses him for some special work which glorifies Him or that God has been generous with His grace, this soul wishes to keep everything hidden. If this is not possible, he is careful to attribute every success to others and to divine mercy. The truly humble person is sincere in acting thus and considers himself the least of all.

3. St. Vincent de Paul wrote, "This humility is the foundation of all evangelical perfection and sets the spiritual life in motion. Whoever possesses this humility will acquire every benefit along with it. Instead, he who does not possess it will lose all the good things he has and will be troubled by many anxieties."

St. Bernard taught, "Humility is a virtue that is always accompanied by divine grace." Humility empties the soul of self-love and vainglory, preparing a place which God promptly fills. "Every valley shall be filled..." (Luke 3:5).

Reflection—Pride is the most stubborn of passions since it is very difficult to change the inclinations of the heart. Only God's grace and constant battle will implant other tendencies within the heart. Do I strive to conquer my pride? Do I pray?

Resolution—My heart must also be nourished by another goal: charity. St. Augustine said, "Nothing is more sublime than the way of charity, but only the humble walk along its path."

Prayer—Jesus Master, I contemplate You in the act of washing the Apostles' feet. You knelt at the feet of Your creatures—at the feet of Peter, who would deny You; of Judas, who would betray You; of the other Apostles, who would soon abandon You.... What a reproach to my pride! And You did this wholeheartedly. Your humility was sincere, not hypocritical; at the same time, it is mysterious! My pride is also mysterious. Time and time again I have acknowledged my many faults, and yet in practice I always expect honor, respect and the first places. Lord, give me a change of heart: "If I then, your Lord and Teacher, have washed your feet, you also ought to wash one another's feet" (John 13:14).

HUMILITY—V

"Truly, I say to you, unless you turn and become like children, you will never enter the kingdom of heaven. Whoever humbles himself like this child, he is the greatest in the kingdom of heaven. Whoever receives one such child in my name receives me."   —Matthew 18:3-5

1. Humility extends itself also to life, words and actions. To *life*: At all times and in every place the humble person lives with great respect in the presence of God and of his neighbor. He lives an ordinary life, not trying to be distinguished, except by his great diligence in the practice of common virtues. He follows the example of the best and what is prescribed. He practices the daily duties of his state of life. His main goal is first of all the sanctification of his interior thoughts and sentiments.

The humble person is obedient and submissive towards authority. He is forebearing and patient with equals, and kind and serviceable towards inferiors.

The humble person loves the poor, the ignorant, the afflicted, children, the sick, sinners and the persecuted. He is a noble-hearted person who understands and sympathizes with them, comforting and helping them.

The humble person loves poverty. His manner is simple and completely natural. He is loved because he loves.

The humble person accepts crosses. He makes reparation for his sins and permits himself to be guided by a spiritual director.

2. To *words:* The humble person does not praise himself. He seldom speaks of himself, and even then he says only what is necessary out of duty. He is opposed to useless, vain declarations of incapacity or guilt, which are often secret attempts to receive words of praise.

He is moderate in his choice of words, and speaks with humility and meekness. He never allows himself sudden outbursts, nor does he speak roughly. He is serious and sober in his ways. There is much vanity in always wishing to speak.

The humble person never passes judgment, especially rash judgment of his neighbor. Rather, he listens to others, and agrees or offers his opinion with kindness.

St. Benedict does not condemn laughter when it is an expression of true joy. However, he does so when laughter is vulgar, undignified and mocking, or when there is the tendency to laugh boisterously and frivolously, since this is a sign of disrespect for God's presence and of little humility.

3. The humble person is moderate in his actions. He is modest and without affectation when he walks, sits, looks about or stands erect. His head is slightly bowed, thinking of God and reflecting that one is unworthy to raise his eyes to heaven: "Lord, I am not worthy, I, a sinner, to raise my eyes to heaven." And if he does look heavenward, it is with confidence in divine mercy.

The humble person possesses the spirit of religion and so is devout in everything that concerns the worship of God.

The humble person has the spirit of dependence, true and sincere.

The humble person rejoices in the well-being of his neighbor and shows it.

The humble person does not seek praise, nor does he brag about goods he does not possess. He does not risk any undertaking without reflection, but in all things seeks the help of advice and prayer. However, if something is for God's glory, he does not let human respect deter him from doing it.

Reflection—These are signs of humility: intellectual docility, understanding toward everyone, moderation in everything. Do I note these signs within myself?

Resolution—I will examine my interior and exterior: my mind, will and heart.

Prayer—Lord, all glory to You! You alone are holy; You alone are Lord. You alone are the Most High.

I shall often bless myself with the sign of the cross of St. Francis de Sales: "By myself I can do nothing, with God I can do all things; for love of God I want to do all; to God all honor, to me the humiliation."

OBEDIENCE—I

"Let everyone obey the authorities that are over him, for there is no authority except from God, and all authority that exists is established by God. As a consequence, the man who opposes authority rebels against the ordinance of God; those who resist thus shall draw condemnation down upon themselves."   —Romans 13:1-2 (NAB)

1. Obedience is a moral and supernatural virtue. It inclines the Christian to submit his will to that of legitimate superiors, as representatives of God.

We were created by God and therefore we are dependent on Him. All creatures do His will: "...All things are your servants" (Psalm 119:91). But man owes God a more perfect obedience. Having been given freedom and created a rational being, he is all the more indebted to God. Moreover, in Jesus Christ we are the adopted children of God. Jesus fulfilled the will of the Father in all things. He obeyed Mary and Joseph and at every moment He corresponded to the Father's will, "and became obedient unto death" (Philippians 2:8).

Jesus Christ ransomed us from being slaves to the devil, and therefore we belong to Him. "You are not your own. You were bought with a price" (1 Corinthians 6:19-20). Consequently, we must obey the Gospel and the Church.

2. However, God does not give His commands or precepts directly. He has His representatives in those who hold positions of authority. In society, families, communities, and nations, in the Church and in every organization there must be those who guide. "...There is no authority except from God..."

(Romans 13:1). To obey one's superiors is to obey God. To disobey them is to disobey God and deserve eternal damnation: "As a consequence, the man who opposes authority rebels against the ordinance of God; those who resist thus shall draw condemnation down upon themselves" (Romans 13:2 NAB).

Superiors obey God by serving in their needs those they govern. They are responsible for them before Him. They exercise their power out of obedience and those who obey them know they are listening to God Himself. "He who hears you hears me, and he who rejects you rejects me" (Luke 10:16).

In a community without obedience, anarchy would rule, and all the members would suffer. One is not obliged to obey in anything that is sinful or contrary to natural or divine law. In such cases, in fact, one is forbidden to obey.

The Pope, bishops, pastors and religious superiors should be given loving and religious obedience.

3. The Lord told St. Catherine of Siena, "How sweet and glorious is that obedience which contains all the other virtues! It is born of charity; on it is founded the rock of holy faith; it is a queen, and he who weds her will never suffer any harm, but will experience only peace and serenity.... Oh, obedience! You sail without effort, and reach the port of happiness without danger!... You are great and your greatness is so far-reaching as to stretch from heaven to earth, since you open heaven itself."

Reflection—Do I understand well the virtue of obedience? Do I obey supernaturally? Do I love obedience?

Resolution—I will remember Jesus' example: "He...was obedient to them" (Luke 2:51).

Prayer—Lord, let me understand that I have to obey always and in everything. Give me this spirit of interior mortification of my will. Help me to understand the merit of obedience and the immense peace it brings to the soul. Let me also understand how I should obey: not because I can see that what is commanded is good and advantageous, but because it is commanded, because it is Your will. Always, in all things, do with me as You wish. I am Yours; I belong entirely to You, with all my being, at every moment. I accept all from You. Lead my life as You see fit. In life and in death may Your will, not mine, be done.

OBEDIENCE—II

"I am the Lord your God,
   who teaches you to profit,
   who leads you in the way you should go.
O that you had hearkened to my commandments!
   Then your peace would have been like a river,
   and your righteousness like the waves of the sea."
                                                    —Isaiah 48:17-18

1. To live joyfully in obedience, and to derive the most precious and delightful fruit from it, this virtue is to be supernatural, universal and entire.

Supernatural: The grace of God is required for obedience, and therefore prayer is necessary. Obedience is a difficult virtue because it has to be practiced every day—rather, every moment. Saint Pachomius declared to a young religious who desired martyrdom, "It is more of a martyrdom to persevere one's whole lifetime in obedience than to die quickly by the sword." To obey each day, we must pray each day. We also have to see God in parents and superiors since they represent God. It is not obedience to accept an order simply because the superior is well-educated, or threatens punishment, or commands gently in order to gain one's affection. Instead, obedience is noble, constant and meritorious when we obey as to Jesus Christ: "Do not render service for appearance only and to please men, but do God's will with your whole heart as slaves of Christ" (Ephesians 6:6 NAB). The more one sees God, the more perfect will our obedience be.

2. *Universal* obedience: Obedience is due to all legitimate superiors in everything which is not forbidden. St. Thomas says, "He who obeys in illicit things, obeys rashly." St. Francis de Sales wrote, "Obedience requires one to do all that is commanded lovingly and simply, without ever considering whether the command is well given or not, as long as the one commanding has the power to command and the command itself serves to unite our mind to God." He further explains, "The truly obedient person will be victorious in all the difficulties which obedience may entail. No matter how difficult the way on which he travels, he will always proceed with honor."

In commanding, the superior may make a mistake. However, he who obeys never does. God sees the heart, and one who obeys with an upright spirit always earns merit.

3. *Entire* obedience: It is the whole person who must submit to the Lord: mind, will, heart and body. In fact, most of the time the Lord asks of us what is more internal and more precious.

Obedience is to be *constant*. It is perseverance that makes a person virtuous. St. Francis de Sales wrote, "To do joyfully what is commanded only once, as long as one would like it, costs very little. But when we are told, 'You shall do this always, all your life long,' therein lies virtue and merit."

Obedience is *prompt*. St. Bernard said, "The truly obedient person knows no delays, abhors tomorrow, avoids procrastination and anticipates orders; he keeps his eyes alert, his ears open, his tongue ready to speak, his hands ready to work, and his feet ready to move swiftly. He is wholly intent on accepting and immediately carrying out the will of the one who commands."

Reflection—Are these my convictions about obedience? In practical life, is my obedience supernatural, universal, entire? Do I pray for this?

Resolution—I want to obey joyfully; only in this way will I be ready to hasten wherever obedience calls me.

Prayer—My God, I adore Your most holy will. You are good, and want only and always what is good. From all eternity You have disposed everything with wisdom and love, also in my regard. You have prepared superiors who represent You and who transmit Your desires to me. I adore Your only begotten Son, always united to You in one, sole perfect will. Your every desire is also our own desire, O heavenly Father, in union with the Holy Spirit. And I, following Your wishes and desires, walk securely towards eternal happiness. Grant that in presenting myself at Your judgment, I will be able to say, "Father, I have never disobeyed Your commands."

OBEDIENCE—III

"Not every one who says to me, 'Lord, Lord,' shall enter the kingdom of heaven, but he who does the will of my Father who is in heaven."   —Matthew 7:21

1. Obedience unites us to God in a continual and habitual communion with Him. By obedience we submit and unite our entire will to the will of God. In fact, we place all our faculties and all the powers of our soul at His service.

Renouncing our will is a sacrifice acceptable to God—in fact, the most acceptable to Him: "To obey is better than sacrifice" (1 Samuel 15:22). It is a type of martyrdom and continual immolation. Through obedience, one immolates his self-will, says St. Gregory the Great. So, if sacramental communion unites us to Jesus Christ for a short while, obedience prolongs this union spiritually. We are in Jesus and Jesus is in us: "Only one will, and only one 'will not.'"

2. St. Augustine says that obedience is the mother and guardian of virtue. Obedience is charity in action. "If you love me, you will keep my commandments" (John 14:15).

Moreover, to live in union with the divine will means to practice all virtues. They are all summed up in obedience, just as basically all sins are disobedience. He who does the will of God is patient, charitable, steadfast in the fulfillment of the duties of his state of life, upright, strong, temperate, mortified, and so on.

Obedience leads to profound peace. The obedient soul knows it is pleasing God and lives happily under His loving gaze. It rests safely aboard ship, knowing that its pilot is God, the good Father. He always arranges everything with love and for our greater good, so why worry?

The obedient person knows that the Lord punishes only one who does not do His will. Therefore he knows that he is moving not towards damnation but towards paradise. Moreover, he knows that all his actions, even the least significant, are transformed into precious merit for heaven.

3. Obedience consists of three degrees.

First: The obedient person observes the commandments of God and of the Church. He carries out the superior's orders diligently, punctually and with a supernatural intention.

Second: He patterns himself on the examples of Jesus, contemplating the Savior in His life at Nazareth and on Calvary. He submits himself wholeheartedly to the divine will, even in the most painful circumstances.

Third: Progressing even more, the obedient person submits his own judgment, conforming it to the will of superiors.

Reflection—Do I realize how many treasures are contained in obedience? What degree have I reached? Do I make an effort to progress?

Resolution—Obedience is a most reasonable virtue. It leads me to do what is better in itself, and what is more useful for me in time and in eternity.

Prayer—Lord, to my nature "obedience" sounds as hard as a club. But I know that in heaven I shall be exalted to the degree that I have been submissive on earth. "Thy will be done on earth, as it is in heaven."

May the most holy, most just, and most loving will of God be obeyed, praised and exalted eternally, in all things. Help me know what would please You today. Speak, for Your servant is listening. Yes, I shall submit my will, heart and judgment generously. Please accept my service and grant me the merit.

PURITY—I

"For this is the will of God, your sanctification: that you abstain from immorality; that each one of you know how to control his own body in holiness and honor, not in the passion of lust like heathen who do not know God."
—1 Thessalonians 4:3-5

1. Chastity is that virtue which leads us to control the immoderate desires of the flesh.

One is the state of the married and another the state of the unmarried. In the married state, what is required by the lawful use of Matrimony for the propagation of the human race is holy. Outside of this, all sensual pleasure is forbidden.

Conjugal chastity imposes mutual fidelity, purity of intention and honesty in relations between spouses. It is necessary to have a very high concept of marriage and consider it according to the spirit of the Church. St. Paul writes, "Wives, be subject to your husbands, as to the Lord. For the husband is the head of the wife as Christ is the head of the church, his body, and is himself its Savior. As the church is subject to Christ, so let wives also be subject in everything to their husbands. Husbands, love your wives, as Christ loved the church and gave himself up for her, that he might sanctify her, having cleansed her by the washing of water with the word, that he might present the church to himself in splendor, without spot or wrinkle or any such thing, that she might be holy and without blemish" (Ephesians 5:22-27).

2. Outside of marriage, everyone must observe absolute continence. This refers to young people, widows, and those chosen souls who are called to a more perfect life and live in perpetual celibacy, such as religious, priests and even other persons of the world.

To control the strong inclinations of the flesh is a great virtue: "The desires of the flesh are against the Spirit" (Galatians 5:17). They are strong inclinations, which can even become extremely intense, if there have already been downfalls, or if one exposes himself to dangers. Among human battles, the most difficult are those against the flesh, and he who fights these more difficult battles exercises uncommon virtue.

Moreover, chastity is greatly meritorious. It renders life on earth similar to life in heaven, which is all pure and holy. It is a pledge of eternal salvation.

3. Blessed are the pure of heart for they shall see God. This is what You taught, O Divine Master. In fact, the pure of heart foster noble thoughts. They cherish aspirations of charity. Their words and actions are lofty, worthy of man and little less than those of the angels.

Reflection—Do I clearly understand the duties of my state? Do I know how to elevate myself to a worthy life?

Resolution—I shall constantly endeavor to elevate myself so that I may live in holiness and grace.

Prayer—Mother most pure, pray for us; Mother most chaste, pray for us; Mother inviolate, pray for us; Mother undefiled, pray for us; holy Virgin of virgins, pray for us; Mother of divine grace, pray for us; Virgin most prudent, pray for us.

PURITY—II

"Put to death therefore what is earthly in you: immorality, impurity, passion, evil desire, and covetousness, which is idolatry. On account of these the wrath of God is coming. In these you once walked, when you lived in them. But now put them all away." —Colossians 3:5-8

1. The Divine Master said, "This kind cannot be driven out by anything but prayer and fasting" (Mark 9:29). Again, "Watch and pray that you may not enter into temptation" (Matthew 26:41). Therefore, three means are necessary: mortification, avoiding the occasion and prayer.

Mortification: it is primarily interior and exterior humility. Before becoming impure, many are proud and presumptuous. "God, who cannot suffer pride in a soul, allows it to be profoundly humiliated...in order that it may recognize its weakness.... He permits it to be afflicted by these terrible temptations and at times also to succumb to them completely since they are the most shameful and cause so much confusion. Instead, when one is convinced that of himself he cannot remain chaste, he repeats St. Philip Neri's prayer: 'O my God, do not trust Philip, otherwise he will betray You'" (Olier).

Everyone has reason to fear: those who have already fallen, because temptations will return with greater intensity; and those who have always been innocent, for a crisis will come to all: laity, religious, adults, the elderly, holy souls and young people.

While the body lives, the devil presents thousands of cunning and deceitful tricks. Humility, which is true self-knowledge, leads us to open our soul to the confessor, to have a holy fear of sin and to pray humbly to the Lord each day.

2. Furthermore, external mortification is necessary. The body must be disciplined and subjected to the soul. "But I pommel my body and subdue it, lest after preaching to others I myself should be disqualified" (1 Corinthians 9:27). Temperance is necessary, and sometimes even fasting or some exterior exercise of penance.

Rest is to be regulated so that it is sufficient but not extra. Idleness is the teacher of much malice.

The eyes are the windows of the soul. Through them enter images and fantasies, and then thoughts follow. Job said he had made a pact with his eyes in order not to undergo internal temptations. Ben Sira taught that one must not stare at a beautiful woman,

"Many have been misled by a woman's beauty, and by it passion is kindled like a fire" (Sirach 9:8).

The sense of touch is very dangerous because it arouses sensual impressions. It is necessary to refrain from those touches, caresses, etc., which arouse passion. Olier said: "Suffer all internal martyrdom and all the crosses of the flesh and even of the devil, rather than touch yourself especially during temptations."

Speech and hearing must also be mortified: all loose conversations are to be completely avoided. An unhealthy curiosity to know things and an unhealthy pleasure in talking are causes of countless evils, temptations and imaginings.

It is easy for one to pray "not to be led into temptation," but in the meantime to go in search of it. St. Paul warns, "Nor should there be any obscene, silly, or suggestive talk; all that is out of place" (Ephesians 5:4 NAB).

3. The Lord is faithful in His promises: "God is faithful, and he will not let you be tempted beyond your strength, but with the temptation will also provide the way of escape, that you may be able to endure it" (1 Corinthians 10:13).

Reflection—Do I have a true interior distrust of myself? Do I practice mortification of the senses? Do I confidently turn to the Lord for help?

Resolution—Since I am not able to practice great penances as many saints did, I shall at least make some smaller mortifications of spirit and the senses.

Prayer—O Lord, purify our senses and our hearts with the fire of Your Holy Spirit, so that we may serve You with a chaste body and may be pleasing to You for our purity of heart.

PURITY—III

"Shun immorality. Every other sin which a man commits is outside the body; but the immoral man sins against his own body. Do you not know that your body is a temple of the Holy Spirit within you, which you have from God? You are not your own."   —1 Corinthians 6:18-19

1. Avoiding dangerous occasions is the second means for safeguarding the lily of purity, or for making up for lost innocence.

Occasions are those things, persons or actions which expose us to sin or urge us on to sin. The Holy Spirit says: "Whoever loves danger will perish by it" (Sirach 3:26).

Mutual attraction between persons of opposite sexes may lead to sin: all unnecessary encounters are to be avoided. The sentiments are a most noble but also a most dangerous faculty of man. Even when they have been offered to God, they remain open to human affection. Grace and firmness are needed to discipline them and keep them in check. Often one may begin with useful things, perhaps even the best, only to end up where one had never intended to go.

If a certain tenderness takes possession of the heart, danger is already evident; if one looks for a person too much, without a just reason, the danger has already been consented to: it is absolutely necessary to put a stop to it.

2. *Idleness:* "Idleness teaches much evil" (Sirach 33:27).

He who applies himself generously to the fulfillment of his duties and responsibilities frees himself from many dangers. A hundred devils would not suffice to tempt one who is busy, while one devil is enough to tempt someone who is idle. In fact, an idle person easily daydreams and reads improper books and newspapers. He indulges in long visits, and chats with dangerous persons. His heart yields itself to sensitive affections, his soul is open to all kinds of impressions, and his senses become arrogant. In working, instead, the mind is busy with serious thoughts, the heart is set on obtaining what is needed, energies are well spent in doing good; meanwhile, the multiplicity of occupations absorbs all one's time.

Temptation assails everyone. St. Jerome complained that even in his very solitude, under the rays of a scorching sun, in the poverty of his cave, he felt himself being drawn back again by his imagination to the allurements of Rome. His advice is to banish such imaginings as soon as they arise: "...Kill the enemy while it is small; do not allow the weeds to grow; eradicate them while they are seeds." Otherwise, they will take possession of the entire soul, and the soul that had first been the temple of the Holy Trinity, will become a den of demons: "Be on guard, so that where once the Holy Trinity dwelled, demons won't dance nor the sirens build their nests."

3. There are numerous and unexpected occasions: books, newspapers, films, radio, TV, persons with whom one lives, sometimes even the best. The devil prepares these occasions with very cunning skill; the whole world is full of them: our body, memory, heart, etc., are always with us. Who will deliver us from so many enemies and occasions? Only the grace of God.

Reflection—Am I aware of the more frequent occasions I encounter? Do I profit from the advice of my confessor and superiors, who warn me? Do I energetically avoid dangerous occasions?

Resolution—I shall meditate on these words: "That which I say to you I say to all: *Be vigilant.*" This advice is given to everyone, and therefore also to me.

Prayer—O Lord, I know my weakness, at least in part. It would be rash if, being such a weak vessel, I should expose myself to all winds, all high seas, and all sorts of storms. It would be an unpardonable rashness if I behaved as St. Peter, who did not yield to Your advice: "The cock will not crow this day, until you three times deny that you know me" (Luke 22:34). How many counsels were received, how many recommendations were heard, and yet how many persons I have seen fall! Lord, make me wise. May I not lose the treasures of Your grace and then have to weep. Lord, I shall always cry out to You: "Save me, Lord; I am perishing" (cf. Matthew 8:25).

PURITY—IV

"Watch at all times, praying that you may have strength to escape all these things that will take place, and to stand before the Son of man."   —Luke 21:36

1. The third means for conserving purity is prayer. God permits temptations for holy purposes and motives of love. He wants us to lift our hearts to Him and ask His help. When Jesus was in the boat with His disciples and a great storm broke out which threatened to devastate it, Jesus was sleeping. He wanted to be awakened. He listened to the prayer of the disciples and restored calm. During the storms in the soul, Jesus wants to be awakened, invoked and implored. Then He lifts His hand in a blessing and His friendly smile restores serenity.

The wise man of Scripture says: "As I know that I could not otherwise be continent, except God gave it...I went to the Lord and besought him" (Wisdom 8:21 Douay).

When we ask Him for help to avoid sin and to love Him, the Lord always answers these prayers and to a sufficient degree.

2. Among the prayers, the principal ones are Communion and the sacrament of Penance. Communion always increases spiritual energy on the one hand, and on the other hand, it calms the agitation of passion. Communion is the bread of the elect which generates virgins. It is the food of the strong.

Confession not only cancels sins of the past, but it also infuses a special grace to avoid all sin in the future. Moreover, the advice and exhortations of a wise confessor instruct and strengthen the heart in battle.

In the second place comes devotion to Mary most holy. This is a great and fruitful means for two reasons. She is the most loving and powerful creature with God. She enraptures and inspires all pure hearts. Thus all the heart's affections become so concentrated on Mary that the attractions and allurements of the senses are felt much less. On her part, Mary with her prayers obtains for her devotee a more serene mind, a more energetic will and a stronger heart. "Hell trembles and the devil flees when I say, 'Hail, Mary.'"

The use of ejaculations is most efficacious especially when one is tempted. For example: "Sweet heart of Mary, be my salvation"; "Virgin all-excelling, gentle past all telling, pardoned sinners render gentle, chaste and tender."

3. Love for heavenly things, for Jesus and for Mary should be ardent, generous and predominant. If it is ardent, it will absorb all other loves. If it is generous, the powers of the soul will be filled. If it is predominant, little by little the invitation to love God with all one's mind, all one's heart and all one's strength will be realized. St. John Climacus says, "The virtuous person is he who has the beauties of heaven so impressed on his soul that he does not even cast a glance at earthly beauties. Neither does he feel the ardor of the fire which inflames the hearts of others."

Reflection—Do I understand how much I need God to preserve my chastity? Do I use the means indicated? Am I in the habit of turning to Mary in all dangers?

Resolution—In times of temptation, I shall make it a point to call upon the name of Mary. I will also quickly turn my mind and heart to other things: for example, to my daily duties.

Prayer—O St. Joseph, guardian and father of virgins, Jesus Christ, innocence Itself, and Mary, the Virgin of virgins, were entrusted to your care. I beg and implore you that for love of Jesus and Mary I may be preserved from all impurity. Pure in mind and heart, and chaste in body, may I always serve Jesus and Mary with a most pure heart.

PATIENCE

"I consider that the sufferings of this present time are not worth comparing with the glory that is to be revealed to us. For the creation waits with eager longing for the revealing of the sons of God."   —Romans 8:18-19

1. Patience is the virtue which enables us to accept sufferings with resignation for love of God.

During our lifetime, each one of us has enough suffering to become a saint. We must always suffer something if we are to be constant in doing good. However, we tire easily and become discouraged in the face of continual strain and difficulties. Even if we had no other trials, these would certainly be enough. Some persons endure such trials serenely, in union with Jesus Christ. Others, instead, suffer irritably, or with complaints or cursing. Still others suffer because of pride, greed or human interests. The person who has true patience enriches himself with merits: it is patience which makes saints. Others, instead, heap up sins and head for even greater sufferings in eternity.

2. *Submission* to the divine will was the secret of the saints and martyrs who accepted the most

painful and prolonged sufferings with resignation and sometimes even with joy. "Not my will but yours be done" (Luke 22:42) was Jesus' great act of acceptance of the bitter chalice of the passion. And Job reasoned, "Shall we receive good at the hand of God, and shall we not receive evil?" (Job 2:10)

The thought of *heaven* has always greatly comforted generous souls in their pain. St. Francis of Assisi used to say, "So much good awaits me that every pain is a joy." St. Paul wrote, "With all our affliction, I am overjoyed" (2 Corinthians 7:4). In fact, there is no comparison between the brief sufferings here and eternal joy; between the little trials now and the inebriating joy of heaven.

In this life, *purgatory* is shorter and lighter, while in the next it is longer and more painful. In His infinite mercy, God offers us the opportunity to pay our debt with divine Justice while we are on earth. Otherwise we ourselves can also search for voluntary mortifications.

The *passion* of our Lord Jesus Christ is a most useful incentive in helping us bear our pains patiently. Jesus suffered even though He was innocent. We suffer, but we are sinners. If we wish to share in His glory, we must follow Him along the painful path of His continuous sufferings, which climaxed in the passion.

The *apostolate of suffering* is the most effective. Let us suffer in order to complete the passion of Jesus Christ for His Mystical Body, the Church. St. Gemma Galgani, St. John of the Cross, and many other saints had a great thirst for mortification and sufferings.

3. There are three degrees of suffering: accepting the cross; living in union with the patient Savior; and desire and joy in suffering.

Reflection—Have I reflected well that suffering is a great source of good? How do I suffer? Am I devoted to Jesus Crucified?

Resolution—I shall make the maxim of St. Paul my own: "Provided we suffer with him in order that we may also be glorified with him" (Romans 8:17).

Prayer—My crucified Master, I understand Your warning: "If any man would come after me, let him deny himself and take up his cross and follow me" (Matthew 16:24). This is the way to intimate union with You and to a relationship abounding in grace. "I will all the more gladly boast of my weaknesses, that the power of Christ may rest upon me" (2 Corinthians 12:9). Along the way to Calvary, perhaps I will fall under the weight of the cross, but I will immediately call to You for You have also fallen—in order to raise those who fall. In You, I place my trust, "for you, O God, are my strength" (Psalm 43:2 NAB).

MORTIFICATION—I

"Then Jesus told his disciples, 'If any man would come after me, let him deny himself and take up his cross and follow me. For whoever would save his life will lose it, and whoever loses his life for my sake will find it.'"
—Matthew 16:24-25

1. It is a struggle to overcome sin and to live the life of Jesus Christ. It means submitting passions and disorderly tendencies to reason and faith. It requires effort to avoid evil and to progress in virtue. It

is renunciation, detachment, crucifixion, interior death. At the same time, however, it is a conquest, an elevation, a new life, a true sanctification, resurrection, and upright self-control. It is an education of the will and an orientation of the soul towards heaven.

Man rejects evil and replaces it with good. Mortification enables us to live life on a higher plane. It is a crucifixion and a putting to death of the sinful tendencies of our natural passions so that these powers may then be used in the service of God and reason.

2. For one who has sinned, mortification is necessary as a penance. Sin is an injustice towards God; penance is the necessary reparation. Sin is an error of mind and heart; it is necessary to rectify the thoughts and will. Bossuet says, "In order to save mankind, Jesus wanted to be its Victim. But the unity of His Mystical Body requires that, the head having been immolated, all the members must also be living hosts."

Sin has deadly consequences for the soul, but penance rebuilds lost strength and corrects bad habits. The Council of Trent states, "Without doubt, penance leads us away from sin and acts as a brake. It makes one more cautious and vigilant, and corrects bad habits." Besides, penance must be done either in this life or in the next, but it is always wiser to work out one's purgatory in this world.

3. Penance can be internal as well as external. Since the body and soul are both involved in sinning, the satisfaction should also be twofold. A

humbled heart and a contrite spirit count much before God. The Psalm Miserere is a classic example: "...A heart contrite and humbled, O God, you will not spurn" (Psalm 51:19 NAB).

Exterior penance is made with prayer, almsgiving and mortification of the senses. Charity redeems; prayer placates God; privations renew the spirit.

Reflection—Am I convinced of the necessity and value of mortification? Which mortifications have I chosen? Do I offer them to the Lord together with the precious Blood of Jesus Christ?

Resolution—If I sin every day, then every day I shall make satisfaction through some mortification.

Prayer—Have pity on me, O God, according to Your great mercy. Cleanse me from my sins and purify me from my guilt. Create in me a pure heart, O God, and renew in me a steadfast spirit (cf. Psalm 51).

MORTIFICATION—II

"Seek not what is too difficult for you,
   nor investigate what is beyond your power.
Reflect upon what has been assigned to you,
   for you do not need what is hidden.
Do not meddle in what is beyond your tasks,
   for matters too great for human understanding have been
     shown you."   —Sirach 3:21-23

1. In what should we mortify ourselves? Always and in everything, internally and externally.

Internally: the intelligence, will, memory, imagination and heart. It is not a matter of destroying these excellent faculties, but rather of guiding them; that is, rendering them obedient.

What is evil is wrong to think of, imagine, remember, love or desire. What is useless is a waste of time to think of, imagine or desire, since this only consumes precious time and spiritual energies.

Mortification teaches one to dismiss evil and useless thoughts, to avoid evil imaginings and to prevent the desire for (or the remembrance of) evil or useless things. Instead, what is truly good and useful is to be thought of, willed, imagined, remembered, desired and loved.

Withdrawing the mind, will, imagination and heart from things that are useless or evil is called negative mortification: "avoid evil."

Instead, urging the mind, will, heart and imagination towards what is upright and holy is the exercise of positive mortification: "do good."

2. The intellect is mortified by discipline. It is given to us so that we may know God and what pertains to Him, His will and the works of His service. Proud thoughts are to be banished. They are an obstacle to faith, a source of unreasonable obstinacy in one's own ideas and a cause of dissension and discord. As St. Augustine says, "There are those who break unity and are enemies of peace, lacking in charity, swollen in their own esteem, puffed up with self-pride, considering themselves great." Contempt for the opinions of others also indicates pride.

Curiosity must also be mortified. It causes haste, disorder and loss of time. The signs of curiosity are: reading anything and everything, concerning oneself about the affairs of others and having an unhealthy thirst for news. Then there are thoughts against faith, charity and chastity which must also be fought.

3. The mind is mortified by applying it to the study and knowledge of religious truths and to those sciences and arts which are related to our own particular duties. It is an excellent discipline to apply the mind to good reading, to understanding the Word of God and to meditation.

Likewise, using our mind to reflect on how to improve our daily actions, to rouse ourselves to charity, to understand and carry out obedience better—all this requires a continual mortification of our intelligence. If one has profound religious convictions, he will most certainly live a truly Christian life. If the thought of man's end, the examples of Jesus Christ and of the Christian truths in general is habitual and felt, then becoming a saint will be easy.

Reflection—Do I have profound convictions regarding self-discipline? Do I discipline my intelligence and wisely control my thoughts? Do I give my mind to God?

Resolution—I want to have only good thoughts, knowing well that intelligence is the first talent for which I must render an account to God.

Prayer—O Jesus, uncreated Wisdom, You have given me the light of reason. Grant me the grace to use this talent in a holy manner. Free me from every vain, perverse and useless thought. Direct my mind to the ways of wisdom. Open it to ever better know You and Your will. Increase my faith so that I may arrive at the eternal vision of heaven.

MORTIFICATION—III

"So then, brethren, we are debtors, not to the flesh, to live according to the flesh—for if you live according to the flesh you will die, but if by the Spirit you put to death the deeds of the body you will live."   —Romans 8:12-13

1. Mortification is necessary for everyone, always and everywhere. Everything worthwhile demands sacrifice. Study requires sacrifice from the student in order to learn, and a good position means effort for the young person seeking it. Every worker earns his wages with sacrifice, every farmer reaps his harvest only after much labor, and every successful businessman worked hard to achieve his goal. Every professional person, every soldier and every artist in his respective field, must labor and overcome obstacles, discomfort and delusions. He who abandons his work is a failure in life. He who perseveres will reach the goal; he will be esteemed and will enjoy the just satisfaction of one who fulfills his duty. Thus it is, and much more so is this true of the priest and the religious.

2. But mortification is far more necessary in the greatest and most delicate work: achieving eternal salvation. He who does not know how to mortify himself will fall into sin: "If you live according to the flesh you will die, but if by the Spirit you put to death the deeds of the body, you will live" (Romans 8:13). The desires of the flesh are turned to evil: to the pleasures of the earth. And yet the Gospel clearly says not to look at what is dangerous, not to desire forbidden things and to avoid the occasions of sin. This means that one must always control the eyes,

hearing, tongue, touch, imagination and heart. Pleasure-seeking companions, immoral entertainment and bad literature are to be avoided.

Only one who mortifies himself becomes better and holy. By detaching his heart from creatures a person unites himself to God.

By mortifying the desire for esteem, honor, ambition and love of riches, the soul can unite itself more closely to God. It can conform itself to Jesus Christ and aspire to acquire spiritual, eternal goods. Jesus Christ tells us, "If a man wishes to come after me, he must deny his very self, take up his cross, and begin to follow in my footsteps" (Matthew 16:24).

Perfection requires a struggle: You will progress as much as you do violence to yourself.

Many souls desire and resolve to become saints, but they give up when difficulties, struggles and self-denials confront them. St. Ignatius says it is necessary to restrain the senses, to combat against sensuality and self-love. Then the love of God will take possession of the soul and penetrate it in all its faculties.

3. I contemplate You on the cross, O Jesus, my Master and my comfort. How could I be Your disciple if I would renounce mortification? I must dominate my pride and sensitivity, my heart, my anger, and my love of comfort so that I may be Your disciple. In silence You admonish me from Your cross. Oh! Help me in my weakness, make me patient, meek, temperate and pure.

"In the cross there is salvation; in the cross there is life; in the cross there is protection from enemies; in the cross there is infusion of heavenly sweetness;

in the cross there is strength of mind; in the cross there is spiritual joy; in the cross there is the compendium of all the virtues; in the cross there is the perfection of sanctity" *(Imitation of Christ,* Book II, Ch. XII).

Reflection—Do I understand the holiness and necessity of mortification? Do I make mortifications with love? In what do I mortify myself?

Resolution—I shall reflect on these profound words: "Just as a lack of mortification is the origin of vice and the cause of all our evils, so mortification is the foundation of virtue and the font of all our good."

Prayer—Lord, instill courage and constancy in me with the thought of the reward. He who denies himself shall possess eternal life. People make many sacrifices for earthly gain, but I am a person of eternity. Heaven will repay every sorrow, even the most painful. Paradise! Paradise!

MORTIFICATION—IV

"Those who fear the Lord will prepare their hearts,
   and will humble themselves before him."
—Sirach 2:17

1. Among internal mortifications those which regard the memory and imagination are very necessary. These two internal faculties are most useful if well guided and disciplined, but are also very dangerous if given free rein.

The memory is needed in studies, in the arts and in the everyday life of everyone—especially all who have to teach or learn. Imagination is the excellent handmaid of intelligence. It is a powerful aid to the memory, a good tool for piety as well as for clarity and enthusiasm in teaching.

However, it is necessary to keep the memory and the imagination from reproducing images, remembrances and facts which cause dissipation, or waste our energies, or lead to temptation and to sins against purity, charity, humility, temperance, justice, etc. It is absolutely necessary—unless there is a true need—to avoid recalling evil done, remembering dangerous conversations, imagining again seductive events, persons and circumstances. It is necessary to mortify oneself.

2. To sanctify the imagination and the memory, applying ourselves with great intensity to remembering the theoretical and practical things we have learned—all this means mortifying ourselves. Imagination and memory serve to strengthen our resolutions, to improve prayer and to place us in the presence of God.

For example, as soon as we arrive in church, we could picture the crib and kneel, together with Mary and Joseph, before the holy Infant. Or we could imagine ourselves on Calvary while the dying Savior gives us Mary most holy as Mother, as He pardons the good thief, as He places His spirit into His Father's hands, as He dies, etc. If with the memory and imagination we reproduce the mysteries of the Rosary, the stations of the cross, the horrible abyss of hell, the eternal joy of heaven, the calm and serene aspect of a faithful servant of God who dies in peace, etc., then it will be easy to recollect ourselves.

Some persons make every effort to remember sermons, or their morning's resolution during the course of the day, or the maxims from the Gospel. Some study Holy Scripture, memorizing three or four verses each day. The beautiful comparisons, inspiring images and edifying episodes often recalled serve to fill the memory and imagination of fervent souls with holy, pure and joyful thoughts.

There are incidents so edifying to impress upon ourselves and to recall, such as: pitiful scenes of the poverty-stricken; examples of the harmony and joy of a Christian family; useful endeavors to multiply good; the devout, hardworking life of the Holy Family; exemplary persons we know, etc.

3. He who controls his memory and imagination will have two good allies in his work of sanctification. On the other hand, he who allows these two faculties to wander unrestrained day and night leaves the door open to the devil and to the most seductive temptations.

These two faculties are more lively, quick and active in young persons, and the youth who knows how to govern them well will receive much help and will make remarkable progress in his studies and in virtue. On the contrary, by giving them free rein, he places himself in the most grievous dangers, such as reading immoral novels or watching bad movies and plays. Bad conversations and wicked examples will leave their evil impressions on the imagination and memory. These will excite the basest tendencies. "Each person is tempted when he is lured and enticed by his own desire" (James 1:14).

Reflection—Am I firmly convinced that I must be mortified in memory and imagination, withdrawing them from what is evil and using them for good? How do I behave in this regard? Do I help myself with prayer?

Resolution—I shall apply myself diligently to the duty of the moment: "Do what you are doing."

Prayer—O God, You enlighten everyone who comes into this world. Enlighten our hearts with the splendor of Your grace, so that we may think thoughts worthy and acceptable to Your majesty, and love You sincerely. We beg this of You through Your Son, Jesus Christ, our Lord.

MORTIFICATION—V

"Listen, my children, to instruction concerning speech;
　the one who observes it will never be caught.
The sinner is overtaken through his lips,
　the reviler and the arrogant are tripped by them."
　　　　　　　　　　　　　　　　—Sirach 23:7-8

1. Mortification also involves the eyes, hearing, tongue, taste, touch and smell.

The eyes must be disciplined, that is, used for good. We are to refrain from looking at what is dangerous. The eyes are the windows of the soul and through them can enter either virtue or sin.

The Holy Spirit says: "What has been created more greedy than the eye?" (Sirach 31:13)

Christ says: "If your eye causes you to sin, pluck it out and throw it from you; it is better for you to enter life with one eye than with two eyes to be thrown into the hell of fire" (Matthew 18:9). At the devil's suggestion, Eve looked at the forbidden fruit.

"It was a delight to the eyes, and...to be desired to make one wise" (Genesis 3:6) and Eve fell. David fell, because on a day of rest he paused to gaze on a person who was an occasion of sin for him.

In the Psalms we pray the Lord, "Turn my eyes from looking at vanities" (Psalm 119:37).

Many think that they can look at everything ...only to find out that they are unable to prevent thoughts and sentiments which eventually cause their ruin. There are also glances which are seriously sinful: "Do not look intently at a virgin, lest you stumble and incur penalties for her" (Sirach 9:5).

We must make *good use of our eyes*: one young man, when invited to look at dangerous, worldly sights, declared: "I want to reserve my eyes so I can gaze at the Blessed Virgin in heaven."

The eyes give us good service in daily life, in study, at work, in walking, in social relations. Not even unexpected noises would make St. John Berchmans look quickly about. After spending a considerable length of time at the Court of Spain, St. Aloysius recognized the Empress only by the sound of her voice. St. Lucian was so modest that pagans were converted by observing him.

2. Taste is a difficult sense to discipline. We must eat, not to savor the food, but to sustain ourselves in the service of God, just as a sanctuary lamp is kept burning by frequently adding oil.

In the first place, taste is mortified by abstaining from what is pleasing to the palate: for example, not eating between meals; not eating excessively; abstaining from wines and liquors with a high alcohol content, which can cause intoxication; ob-

observing the fasts, or at least the abstinences prescribed by the Church. We should always make some little mortification, even if of only one bite of food. We can mortify ourselves by taking something not too pleasing to the taste, such as medicine, or those foods which are good for us, but which we do not like.

Pleasure is not forbidden; however it is a means, not an end. St. Jerome fasted in order better to understand difficult passages of Scripture. St. Vincent de Paul said that mortification of the palate is the "ABC's" of perfection. The *Imitation of Christ* teaches, "Control the palate and it will be easier for you to control all other tendencies of the flesh."

Reflection—Do I have a clear concept of mortification of the eyes and palate? Do I know how to control these senses? Do I ask the Lord to guard me?

Resolution—"Control the palate." I have made a pact with my eyes in order to keep away even the thought of dangerous persons.

Prayer—O Lord, mercifully govern Your family, so that, through Your goodness, it may be regulated in body and, through Your grace, guarded in soul. O Lord, benignly instill Your grace into our hearts: so that as we abstain from excessive food, so may we also mortify the other senses in regard to all that is harmful to the spirit.

MORTIFICATION—VI

"Be not rash with your mouth, nor let your heart be hasty to utter a word before God, for God is in heaven, and you upon earth; therefore let your words be few."

—Ecclesiastes 5:2

1. To make and listen to uplifting conversations are mortifications of the tongue and ears.

The tongue is mortified by speaking at the proper time. If exaggerated chatter is bad, so is a morbid silence which makes social and community life heavy. It is also necessary to pray vocally: Rosaries, morning and evening prayers, sacred hymns, etc.

Wholesome conversations edify one's neighbors as well as the speaker. As the members of the body are developed by exercise, so is the soul by good, uplifting conversations. Good conversations render one more recollected: "Did not our hearts burn within us while he talked to us on the road, while he opened to us the scriptures?" (Luke 24:32) A good conversation sometimes does more good than a sermon.

Let the tongue speak sufficiently in accusing sins in the confessional; let it admit an error sincerely and make known doubts, temptations and difficulties to the spiritual director and to the one who is able to enlighten and comfort us: all these are precious mortifications of the tongue.

It is also mortification to be silent when silence is appropriate. "If any one thinks he is religious, and does not bridle his tongue..., this man's religion is vain. ...The tongue is a fire. The tongue is an unrighteous world among our members" (James 1:26; 3:6). One must absolutely avoid all conversations and songs which are suggestive. They can even be a source of real scandal. "Their throat is an open sepulchre" (Psalm 5:9).

Let us avoid grumbling. If it is aimed against younger people or peers, it disrupts charity; if it is against superiors, it also destroys obedience. Often those who have more defects are those who do not examine themselves, but they criticize, murmur against and *calumniate* others. Let us avoid the excesses of those who want to talk all the time: "Let not the slanderer be established in the land" (Psalm 140:1). "When words are many, transgression is not lacking" (Proverbs 10:19).

Let us avoid praising ourselves, speaking hurriedly, relating anything which might discourage, distract, or upset our neighbor.

2. The sense of hearing is mortified by listening at the proper time, and even when we would rather not listen, for the love of God. It is a duty to listen to the word of God. "My sheep hear my voice" (John 10:27). "So faith comes from what is heard, and what is heard comes by the preaching of Christ" (Romans 10:17).

It is wisdom and mortification to listen to the advice of the confessor, of parents and wise persons, of the doctor, etc. The same is true about paying attention to orders given and listening to good discussions and the explanations of teachers. To be considered friends of St. John Berchmans or St. Aloysius, it was necessary to correct them! Corrections are to be welcomed as healthful medicine. We must not listen to evil things even if they are pleasing. We should avoid giving ear to any criticism concerning our neighbor or to words that praise us, as well as to bad discussions or news which distracts us from our duties and from virtue.

Some people are very curious and lose much precious time in listening to discussions, news and songs which harm the spirit.

Reflection—Deaf-mutes will not have to render an account to God for the use of their speech and hearing. But am I grateful to God for having given me these two senses? Do I use them well? Do I know how to control and discipline them?

Resolution—I will keep careful watch over my tongue and hearing, aware of the good or evil they can do.

Prayer—I thank You, O Lord, that I was not born deaf and mute. However, I realize that original sin made the discipline of the senses difficult. Help me with Your grace, O Lord, since the redemption You accomplished has remedied the harm caused by sin. "Set a guard over my mouth, O Lord, keep watch over the door of my lips" (Psalm 141:3). "O Lord, open my lips, and my mouth shall show forth your praise" (Psalm 51:15). Your sheep, Lord, are recognized by this: they listen to Your voice. Therefore, speak to me, O Lord, so that I, Your servant and sheep, will listen to You.

MORTIFICATION—VII

"Therefore lift your drooping hands and strengthen your weak knees, and make straight paths for your feet, so that what is lame may not be put out of joint but rather be healed. Strive for peace with all men, and for the holiness without which no one will see the Lord. See to it that no one fail to obtain the grace of God; that no 'root of bitterness' spring up and cause trouble, and by it the many become defiled."   —Hebrews 12:12-15

1. Modesty is a continual and general mortification, especially where the sense of touch is concerned. It is the virtue which controls the movements and actions of the body, so that they may be performed decently and honestly, in serious matters as well as in humorous ones. It regulates one's whole exterior in times of relaxation and in serious occupations. It is a dignified, honest and fitting manner of doing things.

Modesty is a great virtue and rich in the sight of God.

It is the imitation of Jesus Christ, who was modest during His life.

This virtue is seen externally, but it is rooted in the depths of the soul. Through modesty, one arranges his whole life uprightly.

2. Regarding *attire* and *cleanliness*, St. Francis de Sales writes: "Be clean, O Philothea, and let nothing on you be disorderly or poorly arranged.... However, be on your guard against vanity or affectation, curiosity or peculiarity. As far as possible, cling to modesty and simplicity, which are the greatest adornments of beauty, and the best means for lessening homeliness...." St. Louis says: "Each person should dress according to his state of life, so that wise and dignified persons will not say, 'You dress too gaudily,' nor the young say, 'You didn't adorn yourself enough.'"

Regarding *posture:* In general let the body be erect; the legs not crossed, but together; gestures, voice and manners moderated; the dress in order. There is a manner proper to a soldier; another proper to a priest; and another to women. A certain behavior is proper when in church, another when taking a walk, and still others when in bed, when with superiors, when recreating, when at school, when at the workshop or when in the fields. Everything must be regulated according to modesty, which is also politeness and good manners. This virtue is a continuous and useful sermon.

3. In dressing and undressing, when alone or in public, the Christian should conduct himself with dignified reserve.

In giving an opinion, in listening to one who is speaking, in traveling, in studying, in recreating with others, one's behavior is to be considerate and genuine.

History tells of an emperor who always used phrases such as: "If I am not mistaken," "It seems to me," and "I ask you to consider this thought of mine." There have been saints who used to give commands to their dependents by *asking* them to do this or that.

Reflection—Have I considered why some persons are well-liked, sought after and desired, and why others, instead, are avoided? Is my behavior regulated? Do I think of the modesty of Mary and Jesus?

Resolution—Each day I want to practice at least some acts of this virtue.

Prayer—O Lord, in Your goodness, listen to my prayer. Make me virtuous in spirit and modest in my conduct, so that I may resemble our divine Model, Jesus. My outward appearance must not be affected or hypocritical, but an expression of interior humility, purity, piety and respect for my neighbor. But it is also necessary to do good works in the sight of men so that they may see and glorify You,

O heavenly Father. I ask You this through Your Son Jesus Christ, in whom You are well pleased.

THE VIRTUE OF RELIGION

"I will give thanks to the Lord with my whole heart;
I will tell of all your wonderful deeds.
I will be glad and exult in you,
I will sing praise to your name, O Most High."

—Psalm 9:1-2

1. Religion is a moral and supernatural virtue. It inclines our will to give God the honor due Him, considering His infinite greatness and His dominion over all creatures. Of himself, man is too small to perfectly fulfill this duty of justice towards the infinite God; but in Jesus Christ and with Jesus Christ, man is able to give God worthy honor and glory.

God is the Beginning and the End; He is the Supreme Good; He is our Creator and Reward. Therefore, He has the right to our interior and exterior worship. We owe God *adoration*, which is shown by prostrating our entire being before Him. We owe Him our *gratitude* for all His gifts and favors. We owe Him *satisfaction* in the spirit of penance for our offenses to His infinite majesty. We owe Him *supplication* for the continuous needs of our present life, and for all that is necessary to attain our last end.

There are many external acts of worship. The greatest of these is the sacrifice of the Mass. This is also the act of social worship, since it is offered in the name of the Church and for the entire Christian family. Other acts are: liturgical prayer, vows and oaths.

2. It is right and fitting that we give God this supreme worship on the part of creatures. All created things must sing of the power, wisdom and goodness of God. They were brought forth from nothing by God. He maintains and provides for them and directs them towards their end. "The heavens are telling the glory of God" (Psalm 19:1). But they give glory to God unconsciously. Man, instead, endowed with reason, owes God conscious glory. He gathers and presents God with the chorus of voices which rises from creation. Moreover, man must also glorify God as Redeemer and Sanctifier. St. Paul declares: "For from him and through him and to him are all things. To him be glory for ever" (Romans 11:36). "If we live, we live to the Lord, and if we die, we die to the Lord" (Romans 14:8). This duty belongs to everyone, but especially to priests and religious. "For every high priest chosen from among men is appointed to act on behalf of men in relation to God, to offer gifts and sacrifices for sins" (Hebrews 5:1).

3. Through Jesus Christ, and in Jesus Christ, we adore God, we give Him thanks, we make reparation for sins and we implore His help. Jesus is the Religious of God, and in Him as the Head we members can fittingly perform our acts of religion. Thus we will acquire much fruit: "He who abides in me, and I in him, he it is that bears much fruit" (John 15:5): glory to God and merit for us. "In order that

in everything God may be glorified through Jesus Christ" (1 Peter 4:11). Let us act in Christ.

Reflection—Do I understand the virtue of religion to the point of being intimately persuaded by it? Do I love the liturgy in its various aspects? How do I participate in it?

Resolution—I am to offer to God acts of interior and exterior worship continuously: life is a conscious glorification of God. "Father, I glorified you on earth" (John 17:4).

Prayer—May all adoration, thanksgiving, satisfaction and supplication be offered in You, with You and through You, O my Jesus. The Father is pleased to receive this from You, because You are acceptable to Him.

A material action has no value unless it is accompanied by understanding. I shall live immersed in You, O my Jesus: I shall think, resolve and act in You. "It is no longer I who live, but Christ who lives in me" (Galatians 2:20). I intend that my acts of worship and all my actions be those of a Christian, that is, that they be Yours. I shall always have Jesus in my mind and in my heart. My hands shall always work for Jesus, and Jesus will always be in my intentions.

ZEAL—I

"We exhort you, brethren, admonish the idle, encourage the fainthearted, help the weak, be patient with them all. See that none of you repays evil for evil, but always seek to do good to one another and to all."

—1 Thessalonians 5:14-15

1. Lord, help me to recognize the talents You have given me, so that I may know how to spend and overspend myself for souls.

The first incentive to do this is man's noble instincts. They are rooted in the depths of my being, like an echo of God's voice. God is diffusive goodness, and He has infused into man a little of His indescribable perfection. I feel that the purpose of my life cannot be personal pleasure. In fact, I accomplish nothing if I attain only a personal satisfaction, no matter how noble. A spontaneous, instinctive force urges me to go out of myself, in much the same way as a plant is driven to produce blossoms and fruit. It tends to multiply itself and germinate in order to extend itself and live on. From this instinct comes the need to communicate one's knowledge, thoughts and sentiments—in fact, one's very life and soul.

First inclination: I do not want to remain sterile. I have to be useful to someone. Willingly I shall make this my principle: "As long as I serve!" If I am not of service, I am a rejected instrument; I am ashamed of myself.

2. *Second inclination:* Life is short; therefore, I must make haste to produce something permanent which will prolong my existence. The tendency to be a parent is in our nature. I do not want to be a false fire, which gives a ray of light for just an instant and then dies out forever; I will not resign myself to die entirely. No matter how faint the trail of my footprints through life has been, at least all trace of them will not be wiped out immediately. May I at least take some merits with me to eternity! Now, isn't the good done for souls the greatest merit I can take with me?

Third inclination: I feel compassion for human miseries: I would like to heal cancerous sores, wipe away tears and bring joy to saddened faces. The light of truth is an immense good; peace of heart is great happiness; and paradise is the eternal good: all these I would like to give, abundantly and always. What joy to see a famished person eagerly eating the good bread I have given him; to see a thirsty person quenching his thirst with water I have brought him; to see a child numb with cold warming himself by wearing the heavy clothing I have given him!

3. My God, You have willed that zeal should contain a reward in itself. Let not Your inviting voice, heard in the depths of my soul, plead in vain with me. Enkindle in me the flame of apostolic zeal.

Reflection—Until now, what has been my compassion for the unfortunate? What do I do now for souls? Do I obtain for myself the joy of one who communicates and leaves some trace of himself in hearts and souls?

Resolution—I must be father or mother to someone. In the end, one who is sterile will have exploited the world and almost violently repressed his inclination to be generous. I shall give my moral and material support to some needy person.

Prayer—Lord, You made us similar to You. Unhappy is the person who instead is self-centered. We are Your children, created in Your image and likeness. "I do not want to die completely." It doesn't matter if my name is not carved in marble. It is enough for me that I leave a trace of myself in some soul. O Lord, let me imitate You in this!

ZEAL—II

"What we preach is not ourselves, but Jesus Christ as Lord, with ourselves as your servants for Jesus' sake. For it is the God who said, 'Let light shine out of darkness,' who has shone in our hearts to give the light of the knowledge of the glory of God in the face of Christ."

—2 Corinthians 4:5-6

1. I am a human being, but I am also a Christian. The sacrament of Confirmation enkindles in every Christian the fire of the Holy Spirit. In the perfect Christian, this sacred fire produces the flame of zeal. If I love my God, if I believe He has a right to homage, obedience and respect from man, what do I think of the way men live? If I am convinced that I must pray "Thy kingdom come," how much sorrow will I feel in hearing so many blasphemies? How can I live in peace, knowing that hundreds of millions of people grow up, live and die without knowing God and without adoring Him? What do I think when I reflect that many of those who know Him actually reject Him, promote wars and live as if God were a Being of no account? They even organize society as if God did not exist, ignoring His rights. God counts on me because He wants me to share in spreading His kingdom with deeds and words.

2. Love for the Church creates apostles. The Church is my mother, since she generated me to new life and trained me at her knees, letting me share in her rich heritage of faith and life. Whatever I have in the supernatural order, I owe to her. I must love her. She now asks me for children. This compels me to defend her against the assaults of the enemy; to

promote her expansion zealously; to make her loved by those who do not love her. No matter how limited my influence, I must work and make her known by prayer, deeds and words. "There shall be one flock, one shepherd" (John 10:16).

Love for souls requires that I be interested in their eternal salvation. I cannot be indifferent to their salvation and still remain a sincere believer. Eternal happiness or eternal fire is not an indifferent matter. If vice is a disaster, I should be moved to deliver sinners from it. If religious ignorance is the cause of all today's evils, I must be inflamed with zeal for catechisms and instruction. If I fully realize that there is a hell and that many choose the way leading to it, I will place myself at the door to bar the way, shouting, "Stop, you foolish people, change your ways and save yourselves."

3. You, O Jesus, my Savior, have given Your blood and life for souls: "...who loved me and gave himself for me" (Galatians 2:20). Should I fear any sort of fatigue for souls? Should I not be able to make any sacrifice? Should I leave hidden the treasures of grace, the truths of the Gospel, the sacraments of salvation which You offered humanity? You said: "I came that they may have life" (John 10:10). "Come to me, all..." (Matthew 11:28).

Therefore the salvation of mankind is the longing of Your heart. If I love You, I will certainly lead souls to You.

Reflection—Do I love souls? And God? And the Church? And Jesus Christ? Does this love inflame me with zeal?

Resolution—I shall often compare my cold heart to the heart of Jesus, inflamed with love for souls.

Prayer—We adore You, O Christ, and we bless You, because by Your holy cross and death, You have redeemed the world. I cannot allow You to have shed Your blood in vain. I cannot permit that the pains of Your passion be useless. I understand that too often Your death has been fruitless: "What profit is there in my death...?" (Psalm 30:9) Oh! May it never be so again! I shall unite my sacrifices to Your sufferings so that souls be saved!

ZEAL—III

"To each is given the manifestation of the Spirit for the common good. To one is given through the Spirit the utterance of wisdom, and to another the utterance of knowledge according to the same Spirit, to another faith by the same Spirit, to another gifts of healing by the one Spirit, to another the working of miracles, to another prophecy, to another the ability to distinguish between spirits, to another various kinds of tongues, to another the interpretation of tongues. All these are inspired by one and the same Spirit, who apportions to each one individually as he wills."   —1 Corinthians 12:7-11

1. Everyone can be zealous. Everyone—from contemplatives to the heads of families, single persons and the sick. Each one can be zealous according to his own environment and his own state of life.

Zeal is practiced through suffering, effort, prayer, deeds, words, radio, press, example, etc. Now, anyone can practice at least some of these apostolates, such as, the apostolate of prayer and of example.

Often there are dependents; at least, one has some
relationships because of the necessities of one's state
in life, one's work, one's very life. We all live in
society. This is also true of contemplatives, who are
enclosed in the cloister in order to be more united to
God, to protect their virtue and to grow in sanctity.
Even if they are dispensed from preaching, they can
pray. If they do not govern souls, they can still
dedicate themselves to the practice of prayer and
virtue. Their merits help missionaries. The Trappists
prepare the best conquests for missionaries. And are
not the sufferings offered for the apostolate even
more fruitful? Jesus Christ is the Savior precisely
because of His passion and death.

2. The apostolate is also a duty for everyone.
For the priest it is the duty of his state. He received a
special mandate from the mouth of Jesus Christ:
"You did not choose me, but I chose you and
appointed you that you should go and bear fruit and
that your fruit should abide" (John 15:16).

Parents must sanctify the family, and they will
have to give a rigorous account of it to God. The
imprint left upon their children will not be erased.

Employers, shopkeepers and managers can do
much for morality, respect for religion and the
salvation of their employees.

All the good faithful, then, are to remember that,
as they received the faith, so are they to pass it on.
They possess grace; they are to contribute to making
it live in others. They are blessed with the understanding of what a Christian and virtuous life mean.

They are to extend the practice of it with the good aroma of Christ. This is an act of equity, if not always of justice.

But this is also a duty of charity and is included in the works of mercy: to instruct the ignorant, console the afflicted, counsel the doubtful, convert sinners, foster vocations, guide young people on the right path, pray for the Church and for the living and the dead, etc.

3. Lord, I very easily forget my duties and obligations, or else I dispense myself from them on the slightest pretext. However, I do not know whether this forgetfulness and dispensation will justify me at Your tribunal. I cannot be at peace simply because I have not given scandal. I must be positively useful to humanity, to civil, religious and familial society, just as I myself have received positive good.

Reflection—Do I fulfill my duties towards my neighbor according to my state? I must fulfill them diligently.

Resolution—Each night I shall ask myself: What have I given today? "It is more blessed to give than to receive" (Acts 20:35).

Prayer—Mary, Queen of Apostles, obtain also for me an infusion of apostolic zeal. O Mother, you who are so concerned about the salvation of your children, grant that I may resemble you at least a little! May I present myself at the judgment seat of God with abundant fruit!

ZEAL—IV

"Only let your manner of life be worthy of the gospel of Christ, so that whether I come and see you or am absent, I may hear of you that you stand firm in one spirit, with one mind striving side by side for the faith of the gospel, and not frightened in anything by your opponents. This is a clear omen to them of their destruction, but of your salvation, and that from God. For it has been granted to you that for the sake of Christ you should not only believe in him but also suffer for his sake, engaged in the same conflict which you saw and now hear to be mine."

—Philippians 1:27-30

1. Not all zeal comes from God. The marks of holy zeal are: unselfishness, discipline and conquering activity.

There are those who seek God and those who seek *themselves*, even in the works of the apostolate. Self-love can be nourished as much by apostolic activity as by material goods.

Through the prophet Ezekiel, God reproached the shepherds of the Old Testament because in their ministry they sought only themselves: "Woe to the shepherds of Israel who have been pasturing themselves! Should not shepherds, rather, pasture sheep?" (Ezekiel 34:2 NAB) St. Paul also complains of the ministers of God who sought their own profit: "They all look after their own interests, not those of Jesus Christ" (Philippians 2:21). "Love is...not self-seeking" (1 Corinthians 13:5 NAB). In speaking of himself, he writes: "I try to please all men in everything I do, not seeking my own advantage, but that of many, that they may be saved" (1 Corinthians 10:33). The apostle of Jesus Christ never seeks himself.

He does not seek *money*. In fact, he spends it for souls. Of course, the apostle expects from his work what is necessary in order to live, but this is enough for him. He does not aim to have an income or to get rich. Neither does he live in anxiety about his old age. He does not select his field of work with only the thought of remuneration in mind, nor is he a passionate defender of his rights. Souls are his greatest gain. He is all for souls; he serves them without self-interest; and he is happy if they save themselves.

He does not seek *satisfaction* of the heart, gratitude, attention or recognition: these are a type of spiritual sensuality. Therefore, he is not discouraged when these are lacking. In fact, if the pleasant warmth of affection is missing, if ingratitude and criticism are felt, it seems that he acquires new strength and virtue, by correcting himself and working only for the Lord.

And if in the end there is nothing to see but bitter failures, he is content that he has worked for God and that he has loved. He has the serene trust that no sorrow of the apostolate will be deprived of the waters of grace.

3. Lord, may I never seek *human honors.* You have honored me greatly with a divine vocation, by using me as Your co-worker, by making me Your minister. "This is how one should regard us, as servants of Christ and stewards of the mysteries of God" (1 Corinthians 4:1). How could I still desire human praise? Would I still wish to seek a place among men while God allows me to sit among princes?

"To make them sit with princes,
     with the princes of his people" (Psalm 113:8).

Reflection—Do I raise myself above human thoughts and interests? Above human honors? Positions? Profits?

Resolution—You, O Lord, are Infinite Good, and therefore You are enough for me. What do I seek on this earth? God is my portion. I shall willingly offer up for You, O Lord, the sacrifice of an affection.

Prayer—O Lord, I condemn all the ambition, egoism and human interest in my zeal. Humble me wherever I seek myself. To You alone all honor and glory. I intend to repair all the vanities of my life with humiliations.

ZEAL—V

"So if there is any encouragement in Christ, any incentive of love, any participation in the Spirit, any affection and sympathy, complete my joy by being of the same mind, having the same love, being in full accord and of one mind. Do nothing from selfishness or conceit, but in humility count others better than yourselves. Let each of you look not only to his own interests, but also to the interests of others."   —Philippians 2:1-4

A disciplined apostolate.

1. The Church, through the Pope and bishops, directs the works of the apostolate in general. It has a hierarchy given it by Jesus Christ. Man cannot change what has been divinely established. In the military service there is an order of ranks and also discipline; each one must keep his place. So in the Church the shepherds are at the head: educators, teachers, lay organizations and individuals in their particular sphere of action are submissive. The apostolate without discipline is a religious form of

egoism. Irrational contentions, jealousies and the desire to command are to be excluded, as well as inappropriate interference, disputes over personal viewpoints, and desertion of a field of work in protest or out of discouragement.

Ever humble, the true apostle is convinced that each person is to contribute only one little brick to the great structure. He is convinced that the merit gained is in proportion to the good accomplished and that he who does his part well will always reap much fruit.

2. To multiply projects, to work according to one's own point of view, to be unproductive because of useless efforts, to intrude on someone else's field of work, to pretend to do something which is superior...these are all forms of lack of discipline. Instead, to work willingly in one's own area, to be faithful to the plan, to avoid all criticism, to have recourse to prayer and to correct with constant patience: these are the characteristics of an apostolate that will be blessed.

Too often there is greater zeal to reform others than to reform ourselves; more insight in suggesting what should be done than the will to do it; greater pessimism than trust in God; more excuses to do nothing than a spirit of sacrifice; and greater desire to work extensively than profoundly.

The apostolate of the laity is the participation of the faithful in the apostolate of the hierarchy. This implies true submission, profound humility and a generous will to follow the directives of the Catholic hierarchy.

3. Lord, give me faith—that I may understand and believe that the salvation of souls is a supernatural matter. Therefore, I must work as if the outcome depended on me, but expect all from You, because everything actually does come from You.

Perhaps I have often placed more trust in my own efforts, ability, initiative and money than in God. Often I have given more importance to results and to outward clamor than to the true sanctification of souls.

Reflection—Am I one of those who spends more energy working against authority than in carrying out the true work of salvation? Or do I follow what the authorities dispose, in loving and active silence?

Resolution—How wonderful are the footsteps of those who spread goodness and true peace! I shall examine myself often to see if all my actions are such.

Prayer—Lord, You crown valiant soldiers. Knowing this, Your Apostle said to his disciple: "Take your share of suffering as a good soldier of Christ Jesus" (2 Timothy 2:3). Even if we die as You and Your Apostles did, O Jesus, Your faithful followers are victorious. "To die is gain" (Philippians 1:20). Grant that this belief in love and victory will always shine before me.

ZEAL—VI

"So, being affectionately desirous of you, we were ready to share with you not only the gospel of God but also our own selves, because you had become very dear to us.

"For you remember our labor and toil, brethren; we worked night and day, that we might not burden any of you, while we preached to you the gospel of God."
—1 Thessalonians 2:8-9

1. Zeal is a conquering activity. "I came that they may have life and have it abundantly" (John 10:10). Jesus Christ says: "And I, when I am lifted up from the earth, will draw all men to myself" (John 12:32). The Apostle Paul declared that he became all to all in order to bring all to Christ.

The world is far from God and from Jesus Christ. Millions and millions do not know about the Redemption. They are still like the pagans before the Incarnation of the Son of God, before He preached His Gospel and shed His precious blood for man.

Among those who call themselves Christian, many millions do not possess the fullness of truth. Among Catholics, many live in sin most of the year; many receive the sacraments rarely and even more rarely listen to the Word of God. The harvest, therefore, is great, but the laborers are few! Onward then, because the harvest is ripe.

2. First of all it is necessary to pray and make sacrifices, because the Savior says, "Pray therefore the Lord of the harvest to send out laborers into his harvest" (Matthew 9:38). Blessed are the souls who offer themselves as victims for this purpose.

We must work in the most delicate field of young adults, because they are the future Christian citizens upon whom the progress of tomorrow's society will depend.

Children receive their first and most profound education from devout mothers. So it is understood that apostolic zeal finds in the family a field of primary importance.

The apostolate well done among men will be more difficult but more profoundly consoling because of the results. In fact, our religion is especially suitable for men because of the nobility of the truths which it teaches, the greatness of the virtues which it inculcates and for the social effects it brings about.

3. O my Divine Master, I reflect now on the great lesson You gave Your disciples who were ready to call down fire on the rebel city, "[James and John] said, 'Lord, do you want us to bid fire come down from heaven and consume them?' But he turned and rebuked them" (Luke 9:55). There are two ways of displaying zeal: one which drives people away, and the other which conquers them. To speak arrogantly, to command with authority, with anxiety, almost with violence, annoys and alienates.

Instead, souls are attracted by goodness, patience and persuasion. Do good to them: this is the way; but do the good well! This is the means for making progress. Lord, teach me these secrets!

Reflection—Do I deal harshly with others? Or do I use kind, patient and constant good manners in my zeal?

Resolution—I want to act in such a way that souls will feel the need of me and seek me out. I shall not bar the way to them with harsh manners.

Prayer—O Jesus, Master most kind, give me Your goodness. Pattern my heart on Yours. I must listen to Your precept: "Go out to the highways and hedges, and compel people to come in, that my house may be filled" (Luke 14:23). But I must also listen to Your invitation: "Learn from me; for I am gentle and lowly in heart" (Matthew 11:29). Humility and kindness are the way to hearts.

JESUS CHRIST THE TEACHER—
OUR MODEL—I

"The Spirit of the Lord God is upon me,
  because the Lord has anointed me
to bring good tidings to the afflicted;
  he has sent me to bind up the brokenhearted,
to proclaim liberty to the captives,
  and the opening of the prison to those who are
    bound."   —Isaiah 61:1

1. Jesus Christ was foretold as Teacher by the prophets. Moses pointed out: "The Lord your God will raise up for you a prophet like me from among you,...him you shall heed..." (Deuteronomy 18:15). Isaiah predicted: "Many peoples shall come, and say: 'come,...that he may teach us his ways'" (Isaiah 2:3).

Jesus is teacher by *nature*; in fact, He is truth Itself, and this truth is communicable. The Son of God created man an intelligent being: "(He) enlightens every man" (John 1:9).

The Word became man in order to teach. Saint Paul says that God had spoken many times in the Old Testament and in many ways through his prophets, but in the end He spoke through His Son.

Jesus Christ is the *perfect* Teacher; He cannot be deceived nor can He deceive. He teaches by word, but first of all by example. Then He gives us grace so that we may believe His teachings and follow His example.

2. This is how He showed Himself to us as Teacher: His doctrine was always attacked, but never confuted. He taught as one who had a right to be believed, as the one who had the right to be obeyed: "For he taught them as one who had authority, and not as their scribes" (Matthew 7:29). He confirmed His preaching with miracles.

He proclaimed Himself Teacher: "You have one master, the Christ" (Matthew 23:10). In fact, He declared: "You call me Teacher and Lord; and you are right, for so I am" (John 13:13).

And this is how they knew Him. Nicodemus said to Him, "Rabbi,...we know that you are a teacher come from God..." (John 3:2). The Pharisees told Him, "Teacher, we know that you are true" (Matthew 22:16; Mark 12:14). "Does not your teacher pay the temple tax?" (Matthew 17:24)

His teaching is the same as the Father's: "My teaching is not mine, but his who sent me" (John 7:16); therefore, it is divine. And Jesus Christ confirmed this with exactness and truthfulness. He is the only Teacher; His apostles are instructors.

To listen to Jesus Christ and to listen to His priests is the same thing: "He who hears you hears me" (Luke 10:16).

3. On the day of His transfiguration, Jesus Christ received a solemn declaration from His Father. He had climbed the mountain to pray. There, He was transfigured: His face shone like the sun. As wit-

nesses to this, Moses appeared, representing the Law, and Elijah, representing the prophets. Both stood for the Old Testament. The New Testament was beginning, that is, the New Law, the new promise, the new faith: Peter represented faith; James, works; and John, love.

And so the voice of the Father was heard: "This is my beloved Son, with whom I am well pleased" (Matthew 3:17); "listen to him!" (Luke 9:35)

Jesus Christ stands between two testaments: He seals the old era and opens the new.

Reflection—Do I firmly believe that Jesus Christ is the Divine Teacher? Do I meditate His words? Do I follow His examples?

Resolution—I will read a life of Jesus Christ.

Prayer—

"Sunday: O my most loving Lord Jesus, give me grace so that I may love You.

"Monday: O my most loving Lord Jesus, I wish to love You, but I cannot without Your help.

"Tuesday: O my Lord Jesus, inflame me with Your love.

"Wednesday: O love of my Jesus, instill in me a gentle yearning for You and a profound humility, so that I may live and die out of love for You.

"Thursday: O Lord Jesus, may I suffer something to imitate Your love toward me.

"Friday: Kneeling before a crucifix—Lord Jesus, nailed to the cross for me, come and live in me, so that Your nails may be driven into me also, and I may desire to be crucified for You.

"Saturday: O my most loving Jesus, You rested on the seventh day. When I shall see Your glorious face, grant that

through the grace of Your mercy, I, a pilgrim, may rest in
You in the eternal joy. Amen."

—St. Bernardine of Siena

JESUS CHRIST THE TEACHER—
OUR MODEL—II

"Rejoice...in the measure that you share Christ's
suffering. When his glory is revealed you will rejoice
exultantly. Happy are you when you are insulted for the
sake of Christ, for then God's spirit in its glory has come to
rest on you."   —1 Peter 4:13-14 (NAB)

1. It is necessary to know Jesus Christ, to imitate
Him, to love Him.

He complained to Philip because the Apostles
themselves did not know Him. "Have I been with
you so long, and yet you do not know me, Philip?"
(John 14:9) The Apostles knew well the physical
person of Jesus Christ. They knew His miracles and
at least part of His doctrine. But Jesus was referring
to a supernatural and intimate knowledge of Himself: the knowledge of His mission and His doctrine,
the knowledge of His spirit and His heart, a complete
knowledge. This knowledge is necessary. St. Paul
says: "That I may know Christ" (Philippians 3:10).
"This is eternal life, that they know you the only true
God, and Jesus Christ whom you have sent" (John
17:3). It is a knowledge which instills faith like that
which St. Peter showed when he confessed, "You
are the Christ, the Son of the living God" (Matthew
16:16). And like that of St. Thomas, who exclaimed,
"My Lord and my God!" (John 20:28). It is a
knowledge which leads to love, to imitation, to life

according to His Spirit. St. Augustine says, "The more you know God, the more you understand Him, and the more it seems that God grows within you...." The interior man makes progress in this knowledge, and God seems to grow within him.

2. To imitate Jesus Christ means to live according to His examples. We will live according to God if we live according to Jesus Christ. One of the purposes of the Incarnation is that the Son of God wished to make Himself our Way and Model to reach paradise. This is why He said, "Learn from me..." (Matthew 11:29); "I have given you an example, that you also should do as I have done to you" (John 13:15). Jesus Christ was the Son who pleased the Father in all things. "This is my beloved Son, with whom I am well pleased" (Matthew 17:5).

By making ourselves similar to Jesus, we also will please God and save our souls. Those who are chosen should resemble Jesus Christ. From our way of reasoning, talking and acting, those who observe us should be able to say, "There is another Christ."

3. The third purpose in the study of the Divine Teacher is to love Him more intensely, trust Him always and unite ourselves more intimately to Him.

Jesus Christ's love for us is shown by the gifts He gave us: the Church, the sacraments, the Eucharist and His very life. He promises us eternal happiness. Love calls for love! St. Paul says: "If any one has no love for the Lord, let him be accursed" (1 Corinthians 16:22).

Jesus Christ must be loved as God and as God-Man. He is infinitely good, loving and lovable. He is our all: "For me to live is Christ" (Philippians 1:21).

Reflection—How well do I know Jesus Christ? How do I imitate Him? How much do I love Him? How much confidence do I have in Him?

Resolution—I shall continually remember: "You have one master, the Christ" (Matthew 22:10).

Prayer—Lord, Jesus Christ, You who are the Way, the Truth and the Life, give us Your wisdom, according to the spirit of the blessed Apostle Paul, so that in following Your examples we may reach life eternal.

JESUS' PRIVATE LIFE—
HIS CORRESPONDENCE
TO HIS VOCATION

"After three days they found him in the temple, sitting among the teachers, listening to them and asking them questions; and all who heard him were amazed at his understanding and his answers."   —Luke 2:46-47

1. Each year, at the time established by the Law, Joseph and Mary would go to the temple at Jerusalem. When Jesus was twelve years of age, He also accompanied His parents to the temple on the occasion of Passover.

After having fulfilled perfectly the legal ceremonies and obligations, they began their return trip to Nazareth. But, unknown to Mary and Joseph, Jesus remained in Jerusalem. Thinking He was with one of the caravans, they kept on traveling the whole day. Only in the evening did they become aware that Jesus was missing.

They returned to Jerusalem and looked for Him anxiously and sadly. After three days they found Him in the temple. He was seated among the doctors, listening to them and asking them questions. The doctors were amazed at His wisdom and answers.

What was the reason for this unusual behavior of Jesus, who had always been so obedient to Mary and Joseph? We can understand the reason from His answer to Mary: "Did you not know that I must be in my Father's house?" (Luke 2:49)

Jesus followed His vocation. A natural father has rights over his children, but above these are the rights of the heavenly Father. The law of God, one's vocation and the will of God are superior to human dispositions. There are situations in which it must be remembered that "we must obey God rather than men" (Acts 5:29).

The laws, commandments, counsels, impositions and demands which are contrary to the Christian conscience do not oblige us, nor should they be observed.

2. Jesus gave a proof of His divine mission. One day, as the only Master, He would teach His heavenly doctrine. Later He would be the Doctor; but now He took His place among the doctors. Later He would ask others to assent to His divine word; here He listened to the divine word and its interpretation. Later He would explain prophecies and give the new revelation; now He questioned the doctors about the meaning of the prophecies. Later, the world would

be astonished at the doctrine of Jesus Christ; now He astonished everyone by His knowledge. One day He would leave Nazareth and His relatives to dedicate Himself completely to His public ministry; now He asserted that He must be about His Father's business. Later He would reveal the highest mysteries, and here He gave Mary such a lofty answer that she was not able to understand its meaning. Here is the sign of His divine vocation. We must try to discover in young people signs and indications which point towards what their future will be. We should foster vocations and form them lovingly. At the same time, without any human considerations, we must correspond to our own.

3. The solicitude of Mary and Joseph in searching for Jesus, who was lost through no fault of theirs, is a lesson for us. On finding Jesus, Mary expressed what her heart felt, "Son, why have you treated us so? Behold, your father and I have been looking for you anxiously" (Luke 2:48). There are those who culpably lose Jesus through indifference, wickedness, or passion. Let us pray that they will feel sorry for having lost Him and that they will find Him again.

Reflection—Do I obey God when I know His will? Do I willingly listen to the Divine Master's doctrine? Do I have true horror for sin?

Resolution—I shall place a special intention when meditating the fifth joyful mystery, in which we contemplate this very instructive episode in the life of Jesus.

Prayer—O good Master, enlighten me to understand the teachings which Your life gives me. Each action of Yours is a guide and precept which I must meditate and follow docilely. Help me by Your grace. Sustain me in difficulties. Grant me perseverance until death. I wish to remain with You today and every day, until I shall be with You in heaven for all eternity.

JESUS' PRIVATE LIFE— HIS OBEDIENCE

"Though he was in the form of God, he did not count equality with God a thing to be grasped, but emptied himself, taking the form of a servant, being born in the likeness of men."   —Philippians 2:6-7

1. Jesus sanctified His private life with indescribable virtue. He is the model for children of all ages. He showed great respect, veneration and love for His Mother Mary and His foster-father, St. Joseph. No one could possibly honor Mary and Joseph as Jesus honored them. No one could possibly show more love and gratitude to Mary and Joseph than Jesus did.

When reflecting on Jesus, the model Son, we must give special consideration to His obedience, which was a docile, loving submission. The Gospel affirms this with simplicity: "He...was obedient to them" (Luke 2:51).

Let us reflect with St. Bernard:

"Who obeys? The Son of God and God Himself. God, who created heaven and earth, who created man so that man would obey Him. God obeys—He who is the Author of every law written in men's hearts, promulgated on Mt. Sinai and perfected in the Gospels.

"God obeys—He who could never make a mistake, who is the law itself and who will judge us on the observance of it."

2. *Whom does Jesus obey?* Two creatures. They were very holy to be sure, but nevertheless they were His creatures and were subject to error. They were infinitely inferior to Him. Instead, it happens at times that subjects have no respect for their superiors....

How long does Jesus obey? For thirty years, that is, for as long as He remained at home. He had the use of reason from His conception; therefore, He submitted Himself from that point. And in His public life? He obeyed until death. He obeyed Caiaphas and Pilate, and His executioners who ordered Him to stretch Himself on the cross. He never gave a single sign of opposition.

Why does He obey? For one reason alone: to do the will of His heavenly Father: "I always do what is pleasing to him" (John 8:29). He obeyed, not because Mary and Joseph were holy, but because they expressed the will of God. This is also the reason for which we are to obey, not because the superiors are wise, good, older or useful to us.

St. Peter says: "Be subject for the Lord's sake to every human institution, whether it be to the emperor as supreme, or to governors as sent by him to punish those who do wrong and to praise those who do right. For it is God's will..." (1 Peter 2:13-15). "Servants, be submissive to your masters with all respect, not only to the kind and gentle but also to the overbearing" (1 Peter 2:18).

What happens in the world? Because of pride and stubbornness, many do not obey. Many excuse themselves from obeying because they find defects in their superiors. Others obey while they are young, but after a certain age they believe they can act independently. Many obey for merely human motives and only in what seems reasonable to them.

Reflection—Have I understood the true motive for obedience? Do I willingly submit myself? Do I pray to acquire this precious virtue?

Resolution—I shall often say:
"Thy will be done,
on earth as it is in heaven" (Matthew 6:10).

Prayer—O Jesus, my Master, Your continual, loving obedience at Nazareth is food for thought. I am confounded at my stubbornness and presumption in thinking I am able to govern myself. How many precious merits I have lost!

Perhaps I have also been ungrateful, critical or openly opposed to my superiors. Perhaps I have considered obedience to be the virtue of the ignorant, the weak or children....

My Jesus, how much remorse I feel in my heart! How far I am from Your examples! In Your mercy, make my heart as docile as Yours!

JESUS' PRIVATE LIFE—HIS PRAYER

"Behold my servant, whom I uphold,
my chosen, in whom my soul delights;
I have put my Spirit upon him,
he will bring forth justice to the nations."—Isaiah 42:1

1. Jesus' private life was a life of prayer. In the holy house of Nazareth, Jesus, Mary and Joseph prayed in the morning, in the evening, and during the day at the hours designated by the Jews for

prayer. Moreover, the great Jewish feasts were observed: Passover, Pentecost, and the Feast of the Tabernacles. The Sabbath, then, was a day consecrated entirely to the practices of worship, piety and charity, in the synagogue and at home: interior piety—continuous union with God, frequent aspirations and supernatural thoughts; exterior piety—psalms, holy conversations and spiritual hymns.

The little house of Nazareth was the most devout sanctuary of mankind. Here three most holy persons competed in praising God, adoring Him, thanking Him, and offering precious reparation.

Prayer is the most important occupation in life. By it, we reach our end—the greater glory of God and our own sanctification.

2. His prayer was *most perfect*. There are religious whose lives are mainly contemplative and others whose lives are mainly active. There are also religious who live a life that blends both contemplation and action. The Church is a garden, and the many religious institutes are her flowerbeds. They have produced an unlimited number of virgins, confessors, meditative souls, penitents and mystics—an entire army of prayerful souls. But the prayers of those three most holy persons were the most perfect of all.

Jesus Christ lived continually in the beatific vision, from the moment His human soul was created. Mary was the most perfect mystic. She had more intimate communications with God and more mystic gifts than all the saints together. St. Joseph was the head of the Holy Family. He enjoyed intimate familiarity with the Son of God and with his most holy spouse. Several times the angels communicated with Him. According to the mysterious designs of God, he was to guide Jesus and Mary, and therefore he was to possess most special gifts, reflections of the heavenly Father whom he represented.

3. It was *continuous* prayer. Besides vocal and mental prayer, there is also vital prayer. To work for the Lord is vital prayer. There was a special mission to fulfill in the little house of Nazareth—namely, the redemption of mankind. Jesus was carrying it out as the Redeemer; Mary and Joseph were cooperating with Him. Their every activity centered around this mission. Therefore, their life was a continuous prayer.

Reflection—Among the many occupations, do I consider prayer the most important? Do I dedicate my best time to it? What degree of perfection has my prayer reached?

Resolution—Every day I will put my prayer first.

Prayer—Speaking of You, O my Jesus, Model of prayer, St. Paul wrote: "In the days of his flesh, Jesus offered up prayers and supplications, with loud cries and tears, to him who was able to save him from death, and he was heard for his godly fear" (Hebrews 5:7). Your prayer was perfect, interiorly and externally. Let me learn from You the proper way to pray. Lord, teach me how to pray.

JESUS' PRIVATE LIFE—HIS WORK

"Coming to his own country, [Jesus] taught them in their synagogue, so that they were astonished, and said, 'Where did this man get this wisdom and these mighty works? Is not this the carpenter's son? Is not his mother called Mary? And are not his brethren James and Joseph and Simon and Judas?'" —Matthew 13:54-55

1. At Nazareth Jesus, Mary and Joseph lived a *life of work*. Mary's work was typical of any Jewish woman in her social condition. The occupation of Jesus and Joseph was carpentry.

One day during His public ministry, Jesus returned to His hometown and delivered a discourse filled with wisdom and holy ardor. His fellow townsmen were gazing at one another in amazement, saying, "Where did this man get this wisdom and these mighty works? Is not this the carpenter's son?" (Matthew 13:54-55) Others were even saying: "Is this not the carpenter?" (Mark 6:3)

During St. Joseph's lifetime, he had directed the workshop. After his death, Jesus had carried on and become the village carpenter. These people had seen Him spend His whole day at work. Many had placed orders with Him, and Jesus had delivered the finished product to their homes and received payment for it.... Therefore, hearing Him talk, they were amazed at His wisdom. "What is the wisdom given to him?" (Mark 6:2)

Jesus was the maker of the world! "All things were made through him" (John 1:3). And do I disdain humble work? Is it not a social plague that so many aim only for lofty professions, disdaining farm work and ordinary labor?

2. Work is commanded by God. Even before original sin, man was to work. He had to guard and work in the garden of delights: "The Lord God took

the man and put him in the garden of Eden to till it and keep it" (Genesis 2:15).

God is most active; He is the first Mover, and man should resemble Him. Life is motion; idleness is death.

Moreover, work was inflicted upon Adam as a punishment for sin. "In the sweat of your face you shall eat bread" (Genesis 3:19). That bread which before you ate as a result of working but without perspiring, from now on will be wet with your perspiration.

Work is a necessity of life. This is why St. Paul wrote, "If anyone will not work, let him not eat" (2 Thessalonians 3:10). It is understood that there are various types of work, some in which one's intelligence predominates, others in which the spirit predominates, and yet others where the body predominates. There are teachers, priests, farmers, professionals, soldiers, artists and laborers.

3. He who is wealthy but lives a life of idleness, though he is able to work, lives in habitual sin. Even the rich cannot spend life uselessly or in amusements. If one has poor health, he will do as much work as he is able to do. By praying and suffering for society and the salvation of the world, one accomplishes a noble and great work.

Work was most ennobled by Jesus Christ. His work was diligent and continual, performed with the right intention and resignation. He implicitly condemned the excessive demands and class conflicts of our day. The social encyclicals of the Popes from Leo XIII to our own times treat this subject and are highly instructive.

Reflection—How do I consider work? With what internal and external dispositions do I carry it out?

Resolution—I shall read and meditate the social encyclicals of Leo XIII, Pius XI, Pius XII, John XXIII, Paul VI, John Paul II.

Prayer—O Jesus, I look to You as the Model of work. I like to contemplate You in Your carpenter's shop, wearing work clothes and intent on sawing, planing and hammering, without losing a minute of time and with Your forehead wet with perspiration. I adore You, I love You, I pray to You. I thank You for the great lesson You give to me and all humanity. Sanctify workers. Comfort us in our daily labor. Instill in us a joyous resignation, so that we may always aim at two goals: "bread and paradise."

JESUS' PRIVATE LIFE—HIS POVERTY

"Take no gold, nor silver, nor copper in your belts, no bag for your journey, nor two tunics, nor sandals, nor a staff; for the laborer deserves his food."

—Matthew 10:9-10

1. The Son of God became incarnate in order to restore all that sin had ruined. The restoration came by means of example, preaching and grace.

He restored the individual by the example and teaching of a perfect life; He restored the family by practicing the domestic virtues; He restored civil society by giving the evangelical precepts for an honest social life and by living Himself as the most perfect citizen. To His examples and teaching, He added grace.

Let us consider Jesus' spirit of poverty.

His was a *voluntary* poverty. St. Paul says, "Though he was rich, yet for your sake he became poor" (2 Corinthians 8:9). He is the Creator of the gold and silver which He hid in the depths of the earth. During His public life, He changed water into wine, fed the multitudes by multiplying the bread and fish.... He therefore could have provided prosperity, riches and wealth for Himself and His family. He is the giver of goods to the rich: "The blessing of the Lord makes rich" (Proverbs 10:22). We understand that the Lord's preference is for a poor life, even in its outward manifestations.

2. His was a *continuous* poverty. He began His life in a squalid cave; He ended it on the hard wood of the cross, a torture reserved for criminals; and during the course of His life things were no different.

When preaching, He said, "Foxes have holes, and birds of the air have nests; but the Son of man has nowhere to lay his head" (Matthew 8:20). Therefore, at Nazareth He had the food, clothing, house and straw bed of a working man according to the time and place in which He lived. And this lasted for many years. He wanted to earn His scanty food and poor clothing with the hard work of a carpenter.

His was an *exemplary* poverty. His invitation to the rich man to follow Him was, "If you would be perfect, go, sell what you possess and give to the poor,...and come, follow me" (Matthew 19:21). He also declared, "Blessed are the poor in spirit, for theirs is the kingdom of heaven" (Matthew 5:3). Therefore, poverty is the sure way to acquire true riches. All of us are to observe poverty of affection.

3. Jesus' poverty *enriches* us. Not only did He give examples and teachings on poverty, but His virtue also merited for us the grace of imitating Him. How many followed Him at the beginning of the Church and in every century of Christianity: the hermits in the deserts, the sons of St. Benedict and of St. Francis of Assisi, and the countless multitudes of other men and women religious who have lived and live in poverty! Many Christians keep their hearts detached from all goods. Many others use these goods in works of beneficence and charity.

Reflection—Did I understand the divine lesson of poverty? How do I stand in regard to interior poverty? In regard to exterior poverty?

Resolution—I also want to be able to say with St. Peter, "Lord, we have left all things and have followed you."

Prayer—I thank You, O Divine Master, for this lesson on the virtue of poverty. Grant that I may love it and practice it according to my state in life.

You Yourself taught that no one can serve two masters: God and money. With the Church I shall pray to You: Keep my heart free. Let me seek first the kingdom·of God and His justice. Grant that I pass among temporal goods without losing the eternal ones. Instead, with present goods may I acquire supernatural riches.

JESUS' VICTORY
OVER TEMPTATIONS

"...Perfect wisdom is found in the mouth of the faithful man. A man with training gains wide knowledge;
   a man of experience speaks sense."

—Sirach 34:8-9 (NAB)

1. When Jesus was about thirty, He left His home and began His public ministry: "Then Jesus came from Galilee to the Jordan to John, to be baptized by him" (Matthew 3:13).

After Jesus was baptized, "he went up immediately from the water, and behold, the heavens were opened and he saw the Spirit of God descending like a dove, and alighting on him; and lo, a voice from heaven, saying, 'This is my beloved son, with whom I am well pleased'" (Matthew 3:16-17).

From the Jordan Jesus went into the desert.

After fasting forty days, He was tempted by the devil.

Let us take note of the Gospel's words: "Then Jesus was led up by the Spirit into the wilderness to be tempted by the devil" (Matthew 4:1).

Then: that is, after He was baptized, after the Father had been pleased with Him and after forty days of fasting.

A soul may find itself in times of greater fervor and still be tempted—perhaps even after Communion; we are never secure. It can also happen that just after having made generous resolutions, the Lord tries a soul to see if those resolutions were really firm.

Jesus: the Incarnate Son of God is tempted. Temptation, therefore, is not disgraceful for anyone; it is not sinful. On the contrary, it is a beautiful occasion for merit. No one should be discouraged because he is tempted; let him fight and win with courage and joy.

By the Spirit: temptation enters into God's designs: for our humility, instruction and merit. It is the wisdom and love of God which permit it: "God tested Abraham" (Genesis 22:1). "Blessed is the man who endures trial, for when he has stood the test he will receive the crown of life" (James 1:12).

Into the wilderness: it is good to escape from the world; but this is not enough. The devil and the body can incite us to evil anywhere, even in a strict cloister, even in church. No one is spared from temptations, even if already holy, even if already old, sick and dying. It is necessary to watch always.

2. Jesus is tempted with a temptation which reminds us of the concupiscence of the flesh. "Command these stones to become loaves of bread" (Matthew 4:3).

He replies:

"Man shall not live by bread alone,
but by every word that proceeds from the mouth of
    God" (Matthew 4:4).

"Then the devil took him to the holy city, and set him on the pinnacle of the temple, and said to him, 'If you are the Son of God, throw yourself down; for it is written,

"He will give his angels charge of you,"
and
"On their hands they will bear you up,
    lest you strike your foot against a stone"'"
    (Matthew 4:5-6).

A temptation of this sort stems from pride, but Jesus responds, "Again it is written, 'You shall not tempt the Lord your God'" (Matthew 4:7).

The third temptation reminds us of the inclination to greed. The devil took Jesus to a very high mountain and showed Him all the kingdoms of the world, saying, "'All these I will give you, if you will fall down and worship me.' Then Jesus said to him, 'Begone, Satan! For it is written,

"You shall worship the Lord your God
  and him only shall you serve"'" (Matthew 4:9-10).

Three are the concupiscences of man: pride, greed and sensuality. Christ could not have been tempted by His passions, which in Him were perfectly subject to the spirit. Instead, He was tempted by the devil, but the three temptations were related to the three concupiscences.

3. And Jesus won, basing His resistance on Scripture. Temptation is an attempt to deceive, just as Satan deceived Adam and Eve, promising, "You will be like to God" (Genesis 3:5). The Word of God, instead, is truth, light and a sure guide. In every allurement and attraction, let us confront what is proposed to us with what God teaches in His Law and in His Scripture. Only the Lord is our light.

Jesus was tempted, and He suffered to help those who would be tempted: "Because he himself has suffered and been tempted, he is able to help those who are tempted" (Hebrews 2:18).

Let us therefore always find refuge in the Lord. "Save me, O God..." (Psalm 69:1). Sweet heart of my Jesus, let me love You more and more.

Reflection—Do I have the right idea about temptations? Which are my main temptations? How do I conduct myself during temptation?

Resolution—I shall remember the advice of Jesus: "Watch and pray..." (Matthew 26:41).

Prayer—You, O God, pardon sinners and do not desire their death. We humbly implore Your Majesty that Your servants, trusting in Your mercy, may be protected by Your heavenly aid, may serve You faithfully with Your help, and may never be separated from You because of temptation.

HOW JESUS FORMED HIS APOSTLES

"Now the point in what we are saying is this: we have such a high priest, one who is seated at the right hand of the throne of the Majesty in heaven, a minister in the sanctuary and the true tent which is set up not by man but by the Lord."   —Hebrews 8:1-2

1. "In these days he went out into the hills to pray; and all night he continued in prayer to God. And when it was day, he called his disciples, and chose from them twelve, whom he named apostles" (Luke 6:12-13).

Apostles are messengers, that is, they are sent. Jesus Christ was the Father's Apostle. He said: "As the Father has sent me, even so I send you" (John 20:21).

Therefore they are envoys, ambassadors speaking in the name of Christ, and they should be listened to, as Christ Himself: "He who hears you, hears me" (Luke 10:16).

"He who receives any one whom I send receives me" (John 13:20). "He whom God has sent utters the words of God" (John 3:34). "It is not you who speak, but the Spirit of your Father speaking through you" (Matthew 10:20).

Jesus entrusts to them the world and all mankind: "Go into all the world..." (Mark 16:15). They will forgive sins and make laws: "If you forgive the sins of any, they are forgiven" (John 20:23). They shall be "servants of Christ and stewards of the mysteries of God" (1 Corinthians 4:1); light and salt of the earth; fishers of men; sowers and harvesters; fathers of souls; shepherds, and witnesses of Christ.

Whom did Christ choose? For the most part, ignorant and simple fishermen.

2. Jesus kept the Twelve with Him to train them for their ministry: "The Twelve were with him" (Luke 8:1). His work of formation lasted three years. To this work He dedicated the best hours and incessant labor. It rendered good results, although the work of the Holy Spirit was still necessary.

The incomparable Master, Jesus, encountered many difficulties. Often He had to rebuke His disciples for their lack of faith. "O men of little faith..." (Matthew 8:26). "Do not be faithless" (John 20:27). "He upbraided them for their unbelief" (Mark 16:14). "O foolish men, and slow of heart to believe" (Luke 24:25). Often He was not understood: when He spoke of the heavenly kingdom, they understood Him to be referring to an earthly kingdom: "You do not know what you are asking" (Matthew 20:22). They held to their ambitions, and as the passion of our Lord was drawing near, they were disputing as to "...who was the greatest" (Mark 9:34). They abhorred suffering and the cross, and Peter affirmed this so vigorously that he deserved a strong rebuke from Jesus: "Get behind me, Satan! You are a hindrance to me" (Matthew 16:23). But the Savior continued to instruct, to correct, to repeat, to reprove, to admonish and to urge them with patience and gentleness (cf. 2 Corinthians 12:21).

What means did Jesus use? First of all, He *lived together with them*: "You are those who have continued with me" (Luke 22:28). He edified them by His example, which was a school for every virtue. By His life He was showing these good, but slow-to-understand men how they should live, and at the end He said: "For I have given you an example, that you also should do as I have done to you" (John 13:15).

Jesus often exhorted them, encouraged them to pray and corrected them. Life in common was a continual school.

Moreover, He *taught them*: "All that I have heard from my Father I have made known to you" (John 15:15).

He instructed them privately: "To you it has been given to know the secrets of the kingdom of God; but for others they are in parables" (Luke 8:10). With them, He shared most intimate confidences: "All that I have heard from my Father I have made known to you" (John 15:15).

In the third place: He *started them on their ministry* with rules, experiments and corrections. He sent them out two by two, gave them powers, corrected them for their vain complacency and promised His continual assistance: "I am with you always, to the close of the age" (Matthew 28:20).

Above all, He *loved them*: "As the Father has loved me, so have I loved you" (John 15:9).

"I have called you friends," (John 15:15) or rather, brothers: "Go and tell my brethren" (Matthew 28:10). He comforted them: "Come...rest a while" (Mark 6:31). "Let not your hearts be troubled" (John

14:1). He promised them a place in heaven: "I go to prepare a place for you" (John 14:3).

3. The *fruit*. At first sight it would not appear marvelous. To the end, they still showed themselves ambitious in their disputes over the first place; presumptuous at the Last Supper; weak in their flight when the Master was arrested. Moreover, Judas betrayed Him, Peter denied Him, and all showed themselves incredulous at the Resurrection.

In the same way, our work as educators does not always bring about the desired fruit. But Jesus left it up to the Holy Spirit to complete the formation of the Apostles: "The Counselor, the Holy Spirit, whom the Father will send in my name,...will teach you all things, and bring to your remembrance all that I have said to you" (John 14:26). Thus, they became strong, profound theologians, full of zeal. And after having been witnesses of Jesus Christ to the ends of the earth, they gave proof of their faith and love for the Divine Master with their death.

Reflection—Do I reflect on the work of the apostolate of vocations? Do I contribute by prayer, actions and offerings within my means? With what kind of spirit do I work?

Resolution—I shall often meditate on the great problem of vocations: O Jesus, Eternal Shepherd of our souls, send good laborers into Your harvest.

Prayer—O Divine Master, turn Your gracious gaze upon the world. Half of mankind does not yet know You; it lies in the darkness of error and vice. Awaken vocations, but at the same time give us good educators, able to form vocations. Sustain them and enlighten them. Grant abundant fruit to their ministry.

JESUS' BEATITUDES

"If the world hates you, know that it has hated me before it hated you. If you were of the world, the world would love its own; but because you are not of the world, but I chose you out of the world, therefore the world hates you. Remember the word that I said to you, 'A servant is not greater than his master.' If they persecuted me, they will persecute you; if they kept my word, they will keep yours also. But all this they will do to you on my account, because they do not know him who sent me."

—John 15:18-21

1. Seeing the great crowd which had followed Him, Jesus climbed a mountain and sat down. When His disciples drew near to Him, He began to instruct them, saying:

"Blessed are the poor in spirit, for theirs is the kingdom of heaven.

"Blessed are those who mourn, for they shall be comforted.

"Blessed are the meek, for they shall inherit the earth.

"Blessed are those who hunger and thirst for righteousness, for they shall be satisfied.

"Blessed are the merciful, for they shall obtain mercy.

"Blessed are the pure in heart, for they shall see God.

"Blessed are the peacemakers, for they shall be called sons of God.

"Blessed are those who are persecuted for righteousness' sake, for theirs is the kingdom of heaven.

"Blessed are you when men revile you and persecute you and utter all kinds of evil against you falsely on my account. Rejoice and be glad, for your reward is great in heaven" (Matthew 5:3-12).

2. There is only one master, but many wish to make themselves masters. The teachings of Jesus Christ are in opposition to those of His many opponents, who constitute this so-called world. Between Jesus Christ and the world there is an abyss. The spirit of Christ comes from God; the spirit of the world comes from the evil one. The world also has its beatitudes: blessed are the rich, blessed are those who enjoy life, blessed are the powerful, blessed are those who demand respect and fear. The world exalts strength, bows to the domineering, and praises vengeance, boldness and deceit. Of the two masters which has a right to our homage?

Jesus Master was speaking to the disciples. Before His eyes were present those who lived at that time; before His spirit, people of all times. We also were present.

St. Paul said: "If I were still pleasing men, I should not be a servant of Christ" (Galatians 1:10).

3. The difference between the teaching of Jesus Christ and that of the world does not simply consist in pointing out a different and opposite path. It also lies in the fact that Jesus gives the grace we need to follow His teaching. Besides, on earth there is joy and consolation in the practice of virtue; in eternity, perfect and endless happiness. When virtue is practiced, the Holy Spirit dwells in the soul. When virtue is possessed and practiced easily, one has a foretaste, a sample, a pledge of eternal happiness.

Reflection—Do I clearly understand that I cannot serve two masters—Jesus Christ and the world? Which of the two do I actually serve?

Resolution—I shall listen carefully in order to understand what the Divine Master is teaching me.

Prayer—Lord, You sent Your only begotten Son as light and revelation to mankind. Make my mind docile, bend my will, penetrate my heart with Your grace. Defend me from all error, from the corrupt teachings of the world. Grant that I may be a light to the world and salt which heals. Heavenly Father, I shall always remember Your loving invitation: "This is my beloved Son...listen to him" (Matthew 17:5).

JESUS' PRUDENCE AND FORTITUDE

"So Jesus answered them, 'My teaching is not mine, but his who sent me; if any man's will is to do his will, he shall know whether the teaching is from God or whether I am speaking on my own authority. He who speaks on his own authority seeks his own glory; but he who seeks the glory of him who sent him is true, and in him there is no falsehood.'"   —John 7:16-18

1. Zeal must be supernatural: it must aim for the glory of God and the salvation of souls. Jesus' zeal was not only supernatural, but also divine: prudent zeal, strong zeal. The purpose of the Incarnation was clear: "For us men and for our salvation he came down

from heaven: by the power of the Holy Spirit, he was born of the Virgin Mary, and became man" (Creed).

Where can we find the explanation of what Jesus Christ did for mankind: the institution of the Church, of the sacraments, of the Mass, and with His preaching, passion and death? In the most Sacred Heart of Jesus, which so greatly loved mankind: "Christ did not please himself" (Romans 15:3). "I always do what is pleasing to him [who sent me]" (John 8:29).

2. *Prudent* zeal. Jesus prepared Himself with thirty years of hidden life. Before speaking, it is necessary to think of what is to be said. Then, as a premise to preaching, He willed to be baptized, to fast, and to be victorious over temptation.

In His prudence He was most reserved. According to the Gospel only twice did He remain alone with women. Once in converting the Samaritan woman, and it was such an unusual thing that the Apostles were surprised. Then, after the Resurrection, when He appeared to Mary Magdalene and forbade her to touch Him: "Do not hold me" (John 20:17).

Jesus aimed to make the fruit of His preaching last by instituting the apostolate and the Church. Moreover, He did not force anyone to follow Him. He merely invited. He did not impose, but persuaded. He wanted a kingdom, but of voluntary and convinced subjects: a kingdom of truth, justice and love.

3. *Strong* zeal. Jesus encountered difficulty from among His relatives: "Even his brethren did not believe in him" (John 7:5). At Nazareth He was

considered insane and they tried to throw Him over a cliff. He encountered difficulty in the ignorant and hard-hearted: "O foolish men, and slow of heart to believe all that the prophets have spoken!" (Luke 24:25) "Have I been with you so long and yet you do not know me?" (John 14:9) He met with jealousy and envy: "He knew that it was out of envy that they had delivered him up" (Matthew 27:18). Even Pilate noted it. Jesus had difficulty with the Pharisees who tried several times to trap Him in His speech: "...that they might take hold of what he said" (Luke 20:20). He had difficulty with the devil, who tempted Him in the desert, who instigated the soul of His betrayer: "Satan entered into him" (John 13:27); and who roused the Sanhedrin against Him so they would condemn Him.

But, at the cost of His life, He persevered courageously to the end, proclaiming His divinity before the High Priest and His kingship before Pilate.

Reflection—Is my zeal supernatural or human? Is it prudent or indiscreet? Strong or inconstant?

Resolution—I shall study the ministry of Jesus in all its aspects.

Prayer—May the Holy Spirit enlighten our minds; teach us the apostolic virtues; comfort us in the imitation of the Apostle of the Father: "Fix your eyes on Jesus, the apostle and high priest whom we acknowledge in faith" (Hebrews 3:1 NAB).

JESUS' APOSTOLATE OF PRAYER

"When Jesus had spoken these words, he lifted up his eyes to heaven and said, 'Father, the hour has come; glorify your Son that the Son may glorify you, since you have given him power over all flesh, to give eternal life to all whom you have given him."   —John 17:1-2

1. The zeal for the glory of God and the salvation of souls gave rise to the apostolate of prayer, example, suffering, preaching, editions, sacraments, works; the apostolate among youth, men, women and the afflicted.

Jesus' apostolate of prayer. If God commanded each one to care for his neighbor, it is because each person—no one excluded—is able to do something for his brother. One can at least pray, or suffer, or give good example. Even the elderly, children and the sick can do this.

The apostolate of prayer was practiced by Jesus Christ from the moment of the Incarnation. Now it is perpetuated in heaven. He is *the* prayer, because He is *the* sacrifice. He is the prayer that is always answered "because of His dignity." He is the continuous prayer, because He always offered Himself to the Father from the time He could say "...a body you have prepared for me" (Hebrews 10:5). He prays continually in the tabernacle: "He always lives to make intercession for them" (Hebrews 7:25). At times He is more a prayer of praise, at other times, more a prayer of thanksgiving. Or, again, He is more a prayer of satisfaction, or a prayer of supplication. He is the Prayerful One: our prayer is good if it is made in Him, with Him, through Him: that is, in the name of Christ.

2. His prayer is apostolic: He seeks the glory of God through the salvation and the sanctification of souls.

The *Our Father*, in its first three petitions, asks for the glory of God, the honor of His name, the spread of His kingdom, the submission of mankind to Him. The other four petitions ask for ourselves: material and spiritual bread, the remission of sins, the protection of the just from temptation, and deliverance from evil, especially from eternal damnation.

In the Gospel a few of Jesus' prayers are noted; most of them are passed over in silence. But Jesus prayed for the ministry of the word for forty days before beginning it; He prayed all night before choosing the Apostles; He prayed in the garden of Gethsemane for the fruits of His passion.

In the Cenacle, He prayed to the Father for four intentions: "Keep them from the evil one" (John 17:15); "Sanctify them in the truth" (John 17:17), that is, in Your doctrine; "That they also may be consecrated in truth" (John 17:19), because faith leads to sanctity of life; "I pray that they may be [one] in us" (John 17:21 NAB), "that they may become perfectly one" (John 17:23)—perfect unity in faith, charity and zealous works; union on earth and in heaven.

3. The apostolate of prayer can be exercised by all, individually or as members of an approved

association. Everything—including actions and sufferings—can be transformed into prayer. Prayer is more powerful if many persons are united in it.

Prayer is more acceptable if offered in union with and through Mary's Immaculate Heart. She asks every good for those who pray, if they make their own the intentions which Jesus has in immolating Himself every day on the altar.

Reflection—Do I know and appreciate the great merit of the apostolate of prayer? Do I practice it? With what dispositions?

Resolution—If possible, I shall enroll myself in the Association of the Apostolate of Prayer. Otherwise, I shall practice it privately.

Prayer—Jesus Master, in union with the divine intentions with which You prayed on earth and pray in the tabernacle, I offer You the prayers, actions and sufferings of my whole life. I implore You, through Your very own merits; I supplicate You for those who do not pray. I pray to You for all: just and sinners, faithful and infidels, subjects and rulers, the healthy, the dying, and the deceased.

JESUS' CARE FOR SINNERS, CHILDREN AND THE POOR

"As the Father has loved me, so have I loved you; abide in my love. If you keep my commandments, you will abide in my love, just as I have kept my Father's commandments and abide in his love. These things I have spoken to you, that my joy may be in you, and that your joy may be full."   —John 15:9-11

1. Love, goodness and mercy are the characteristics of Jesus. His most tender concern is directed towards the weak and needy: sinners, children, the poor, the suffering.

Sinners. The Son of God became man to save man, lost through sin. This is expressly stated in the Gospel: "Those who are well have no need of a physician, but those who are sick" (Mark 2:17). "For I came not to call the righteous, but sinners" (Matthew 9:13).

They accused Him of being too familiar with publicans. But Jesus narrated three parables to show His particular mission: the stories of the prodigal son, the lost sheep and the lost coin. His conduct with the Samaritan, with Magdalene, with the adulteress, with Peter, with Zacchaeus, with Matthew and even with Judas, is very moving. He instituted the sacrament of Reconciliation so that all men at all times would find in His heart an ocean of mercy.

2. *Children.* Jesus declared that each one of them is accompanied by an angel. He threatened great punishment to those who would scandalize them: "It would be better for him if a great millstone were hung round his neck and he were thrown into the sea" (Mark 9:42). He put Himself in their place and considered as done to Him what was done to them: "Truly, I say to you, as you did it to one of the least of these my brethren, you did it to me" (Matthew 25:40). Jesus Himself had become a child: "For to us a child is born" (Isaiah 9:6). He would gather around Himself the little ones who were attracted by His goodness. They certainly must have been noisy around Him if the Apostles scolded them

and pushed them away. But Jesus defended them and called them back: "Let the little children come to me, do not hinder them" (Mark 10:14), declaring them worthy of heaven: "To such belongs the kingdom of heaven" (Matthew 19:14). In fact, He held them up as a model for adults: "Unless you turn and become like children, you will never enter the kingdom of heaven" (Matthew 18:3).

3. *The Poor.* Jesus made Himself poor: "Though he was rich...he became poor" (2 Corinthians 8:9). He stated that He was sent to evangelize the poor in a special way: "The Spirit of the Lord is upon me...to preach good news to the poor" (Luke 4:18). The first beatitude is directed to the poor: "Blessed are the poor in spirit, for theirs is the kingdom of heaven" (Matthew 5:3). He recommended them to the charity of the wealthy, stating that He considered charity given to them as given to Himself: "I was hungry and you gave me food" (Matthew 25:35); "He who has two coats, let him share with him who has none; and he who has food, let him do likewise" (Luke 3:11). He Himself multiplied bread in order to feed those who had followed Him for days.

Reflection—Is my heart inclined to mercy? What are my dispositions towards sinners, children, the poor? How do I treat them?

Resolution—I shall be compassionate and charitable towards sinners and the poor. I shall be gentle and loving towards children.

Prayer—Heart of Jesus, burning with love for us, inflame our hearts with love for You. Heart of Jesus, ardent furnace of charity, Heart of Jesus, full of goodness and love, Heart of Jesus, abyss of all virtues, have mercy on us.

JESUS' COMPASSION
FOR THE SUFFERING
AND HIS ESTEEM FOR WOMEN

"He shall not judge by what his eyes see, or decide by what his ears hear; but with righteousness he shall judge the poor, and decide with equity for the meek of the earth; and he shall smite the earth with the rod of his mouth, and with the breath of his lips he shall slay the wicked."

—Isaiah 11:3-4

1. *Jesus' compassion for the suffering.* Jesus was the man of sorrows: "He was despised and rejected by man" (Isaiah 53:3a). He knew well what suffering was: "A man of sorrows and acquainted with grief" (Isaiah 53:3b). He was the great Comforter.

He cured many sick people. To the messengers sent by John the Baptist, who asked Him who He was, He answered: "Go and tell John what you hear and see: the blind receive their sight and the lame walk, lepers are cleansed and the deaf hear, and the dead are raised up" (Matthew 11:5). He healed Peter's mother-in-law, who had a fever; cured the woman suffering from a hemorrhage; cleansed the lepers; made the paralytic at the pool walk; and comforted everyone with words of faith and hope. He took our afflictions upon Himself and gave us the true comforts of heavenly grace and spiritual joys.

2. *Jesus' esteem for women.* He brought back woman to her dignity of helper and companion of man. Paganism had reduced women to profound humiliation. He rehabilitated Magdalene, the adulteress and the Samaritan woman to the point of making them holy souls and apostles.

First of all, Jesus became the Son of a woman: "God sent forth his Son, born of woman" (Galatians 4:4).

He consecrated marriage by intervening at Cana: He was pleased to derive parables from weddings to remind us of paradise: "[They] took their lamps and went to meet the bridegroom" (Matthew 25:1); "Come to the marriage feast" (Matthew 22:4).

When one mother mourned her dead son, He consoled her by the miracle of raising him from the dead. He listened to the mother who begged help for her daughter possessed by the devil. He described the joy of a woman when she becomes a mother.

He loved Lazarus and was pleased to work a miracle in order to console his two sisters, Martha and Mary, who were mourning him.

The angel entrusted the pious women with the charge of announcing to the Apostles that Jesus had risen: "Go quickly and tell his disciples that he has risen from the dead" (Matthew 28:7).

Jesus gave this same mission to Mary Magdalene, indicating that woman has great duties in society.

During His apostolic journeys, Jesus chose some virtuous women as His faithful followers. Among them there were mothers of some of the Apostles who became apostles themselves.

3. The love of Jesus was the truest love. He gave gratuitously and recommended His disciples to do likewise: "You received without pay, give without pay" (Matthew 10:8). Material gain, ambition and natural attraction were excluded from His ministry. Therefore, He condemned the Pharisees for their vanity in doing good: "...that they may be praised

by men" (Matthew 6:2). In the end, they would be sadly disillusioned: "They have their reward" (Matthew 6:2).

After the most admirable episodes in His life, He commanded silence: "Tell no one the vision" (Matthew 17:9). After the multiplication of bread, they wanted to proclaim Him King, but He "withdrew again to the hills by himself" (John 6:15).

As His life was gradually drawing to a close, His poverty was more and more evident: He lived on alms, not even keeping them for Himself, but turning them over to Judas, who, ironically, was a thief.

He died naked on a cross.

Reflection—Do I understand sorrow and poverty? Do I know how to suffer something for my neighbor? Do I respect and know how to sanctify woman in her various states of daughter, wife, widow and apostle?

Resolution—I shall often consider the words of Jesus: "I came that they may have life, and have it abundantly" (John 10:10).

Prayer—O Lord, You wished to restore the fallen world by means of Your only Son. By Your grace, enlighten us to know His spirit and His works. Grant us, through His merits, to imitate Him in His ministry, so that we may receive the reward of the apostolate.

JESUS OUR SAVIOR: MODEL OF SUFFERING

"For this reason the Father loves me, because I lay down my life, that I may take it again. No one takes it from me, but I lay it down of my own accord. I have power to lay it down, and I have power to take it again."

—John 10:17-18

1. Christ suffered voluntarily. His was not a simple resignation, as it would be in our case. He took upon Himself a body in order to be able to suffer and die, since as God He could neither suffer nor die.

We feel pain because we are weak. He tasted pain because He wanted to. His soul always enjoyed eternal beatitude: but Jesus found an admirable way to feel spasms of pain both in His spirit and in His body. St. Augustine says: His sufferings are real because in His power He wanted to feel them. In His power He chose the time that He would suffer and the torments that His members would undergo.

The Nazarenes had attempted to throw Him down from the mountain on which their city was built, but His hour had not yet come. So He calmly passed through their midst and went away. The Jews would have stoned Him because He claimed to be God, but Jesus did not will to die at that time, nor to be stoned. So He drew away from them and the stones dropped from the hands of His enemies.

When the appointed time came, knowing that Judas would be waiting to bring the cohort to Gethsemane, Jesus went there. As the band of soldiers arrived, Jesus said to the Apostles, "Rise, let us be going; see, my betrayer is at hand" (Mark 14:42).

2. He willed to die the most humiliating kind of death. To show that He was delivering Himself into the hands of His enemies voluntarily, at Gethsem-

ane, He questioned the soldiers: "'Whom do you seek?' They answered him, 'Jesus of Nazareth.' Jesus said to them, 'I am he'" (John 18:4-5). At these words they fell to the ground, nor could they rise again until He gave His consent. St. Augustine says that in forcing them to fall, He showed His power; in permitting them to rise again, He showed His free will to go to die.

If He had wished to free Himself, it would have sufficed to ask His Father to send legions of angels. This is what He told Peter, who was ready to defend Him with a sword. In fact, it would have been enough for Him to use His miraculous power. He could not only have freed Himself from death, but He could also have raised the others and raised Himself. In fact, after three days in the tomb, He, who had died, easily freed Himself from the stone and from the soldiers who were on guard, leaving them terrified.

Jesus delivered Himself into the hands of His enemies: He accepted the signal Judas gave with a kiss and declared: "This is your hour, and the power of darkness" (Luke 22:53).

3. From the moment of the Incarnation, Jesus had longed for this hour and had offered Himself as a victim. This mission was present to Him all His life: "I have a baptism to be baptized with; and how I am constrained until it is accomplished!" (Luke 12:50) He felt a great desire to reach the moment of this baptism of blood. To Peter, who did not want to hear Him speak about it, He responded severely, "Get behind me, Satan! You are a hindrance to me" (Matthew 16:23). He had to await His hour; but when

this hour arrived, He was ready: "Rise, let us be going!" (Matthew 26:46)

Reflection—Do I accept the pains which accompany my mission and assignments? Do I desire them? Do I prepare myself with prayer? Do I have the interior dispositions of Jesus?

Resolution—I shall meditate on these words: "Christ...suffered for you, leaving you an example, that you should follow in his steps" (1 Peter 2:21).

Prayer—O Jesus, martyrs would die for You, so You made Yourself the chief of Martyrs, as You made Yourself the chief of the Apostles, virgins and confessors.

See how reluctantly I follow You to the cross—limping, sad, almost rebellious. Because of this, I often do not correspond fully to my vocation. Suffering frightens me. O passion of Christ, comfort me. Through Your will and divine acceptance of suffering, strengthen me. Mercifully guard and assist me.

JESUS HONORED MARY, HIS MOTHER

"Mary said to the angel, 'How can this be since I do not know man?' The angel answered her: 'The Holy Spirit will come upon you and the power of the Most High will overshadow you; hence, the holy offspring to be born will be called Son of God.'"   —Luke 1:34-35 (NAB)

1. In His decree of creation, God foresaw Mary as the masterpiece of His omnipotence and love: "Ages ago I was set up,
  at the first, before the beginning of the earth" (Proverbs 8:23).

There is a hierarchy of beings according to their perfection; Mary is at the summit because of her excelling gifts of nature and grace. The Father, the Son and the Holy Spirit enriched her and made her Queen of all creation.

2. Mary is designated in the decree of the Incarnation and of the Redemption as the Mother of the Savior. It is God Himself who said of her: "I will put enmity between you and the woman,
    and between your seed and her seed;
he shall bruise your head,
    and you shall bruise his heel" (Genesis 3:15).

Isaiah describes her as God's marvel: Mother and Virgin: "The virgin shall be with child, and bear a son, and shall name him Immanuel" (Isaiah 7:14 NAB).

Scripture speaks of Mary: "There shall come forth a shoot from the stump of Jesse, and a branch shall grow out of his roots" (Isaiah 11:1).

In the Old Testament we find the most beautiful figures of Mary: the olive, the rose, the lily, the sun, Esther, the ark of the Covenant, the ark of Noah and the staff of Aaron.

In the New Testament we contemplate Mary adoring the Son of God Incarnate, to whom she had given birth. The all-powerful God who created everything was supported by Mary's hands. He who governs and guides the world by His providence, depended on His mother for milk and was carried in her arms.

3. Let us imitate the Lord as most affectionate children. If God has so honored Mary, let us honor

her also. Let us honor her as the beloved daughter of the Father, as the Mother of the divine Son, as the Spouse of the Holy Spirit.

Reflection—Do I know Mary well? Do I read about, listen to and meditate on her greatness and privileges? Do I feel that imitating Mary means lifting myself to God and pleasing Him? In prayer do I rely on her intercession?

Resolution—I shall keep Mary in my mind, Mary in my heart, Mary in my life.

Prayer—O Lord, Jesus Christ, You gave us as Mother, Your own Mother, Mary, and gifted her with great power and mercy. Grant us this grace: always to have our mind and heart turned towards her in life, and especially in death, so that through her intercession we may obtain the fruits of Your abundant redemption.

MARY'S LIFE
OF INTIMATE UNION WITH JESUS

"My beloved has gone down to his garden,
   to the beds of spice,
to pasture his flock in the gardens,
   and to gather lilies.
I am my beloved's and my beloved is mine;
   he pastures his flock among the lilies."

—Song of Songs 6:2-3

1. One who loves desires the loved one, enjoys his company and fulfills his wishes.

The spouse of the Song of Songs was searching everywhere for her beloved, prolonging the joy of his closeness, studying and satisfying all his desires. This was a figure of what Mary did for Jesus when He was a baby, a child, a young man and an adult at

Nazareth. This loving attitude of Mary is a lesson for us: to seek Jesus in the Eucharist; to prolong our conversations with Him; to correspond to the desires and inspirations which come to us from Him dwelling in the tabernacle.

2. The life of Mary at Nazareth was a life of intimate union with her Son. These two most holy persons sought each other. Mary's nearness to Jesus gained for her a continual increase of love, joy and virtue. Night and day, meals and work, prayer, silence and holy conversations—all were continuous incentives to grow in love. They were for Mary daily occasions of ever greater light and perfection, as she followed the examples of Jesus.

The Son was growing in wisdom, age and grace before God and men; His Mother was living in a kind of holy competition; she strove to progress moment by moment.

In all things Jesus obeyed and pleased His Mother; in all things His Mother guessed her Son's desires; at every instant Son and Mother together sought the glory of God and the salvation of the world.

3. Souls who really love Jesus seek Him in church. They visit and adore Him. They thank Him and make reparation. They offer themselves and make supplication before the holy tabernacle. Jesus speaks to the soul, communicating His desires and His love. He draws the soul ever closer to Himself and establishes a habitual and marvelous union with it.

Frequent visits to Jesus are a preparation for that eternal dwelling with Him who is beatitude Itself.

Reflection—Do I visit the Blessed Sacrament? Reverently? With benefit?

Resolution—If it is the delight of Jesus to be with men, I must be delighted to stay with Jesus.

Prayer—O Mary, model of fervent, loving and adoring souls, I ask you for three precious graces: to know Jesus hidden in the tabernacle; to seek His presence in holy intimacy; and to live habitually with my heart turned towards Him.

MARY, THE COMPANION OF CHRIST

"My sheep hear my voice, and I know them, and they follow me; and I give them eternal life, and they shall never perish, and no one shall snatch them out of my hand. My Father, who has given them to me, is greater than all, and no one is able to snatch them out of the Father's hand."   —John 10:27-29

1. St. Epiphanius says, "Mary was the constant companion of Christ and was never separated from His company. She was associated to her Son from the first announcement of the Redemption: in his private life, public life, sorrowful life and glorious life."

There followed [Jesus] a great multitude of... women..." (Luke 23:27). Instinctively they must have gathered around Mary as the twelve Apostles and the disciples gathered around Jesus. She was a symbol of union between those women and Jesus; she introduced them to the lofty Gospel message; she was the first to listen to Jesus and serve Him; at the same time she remained hidden as much as possible.

2. Mary's manner was modest; her speech, moderate and humble. Her hiddenness, her spirit of sacrifice and her dignity were admirable. Mary's life appeared to everyone to be the faithful echo of the words of Jesus; or rather, the living Gospel. Thus she also became, within the limits of her condition, the conqueror of souls through the apostolate of prayer, of example and of word. Jesus acted in public; Mary, as the heart of the Church, hidden and active, in secret. Both Jesus and Mary lived for the service and the redemption of humanity.

3. Behold the mission of the Catholic laity and, in a particular way, that of the woman.

There is the apostolate of interior life: a holy person brings to the Mystical Body of Jesus Christ a pure and vivifying blood.

There are also the apostolates of holy desires and of prayer; the apostolate of good example, which impresses others silently and makes God felt on earth; the apostolate of suffering, which seals and gives effectiveness to every other apostolate; and the apostolate of cooperation with the zeal of the clergy.

Reflection—Do I live with the Church? Do I accompany the Church in her activities?

Resolution—I want to live in the Church, with the Church, for the Church as a member of her body.

Prayer—O Mary, you who carried in your arms the newborn Church, give me your spirit, that I may follow you in the virtue you exercised during the public life of Jesus. May the actions of apostolic laity in the Church be humble, generous and constant. Bless all those who love and work with and for the Church in the various apostolates.

MARY'S BOUNDLESS CARE FOR HER CHILDREN

"This, the first of his signs, Jesus did at Cana in Galilee, and manifested his glory; and his disciples believed in him."   —John 2:11

1. One of the first episodes in the Divine Master's public life is the wedding feast at Cana. Jesus and His disciples were invited, and so was Mary, Jesus' Mother.

In this narrative we see Mary's attentiveness to the needs of others. She is at the wedding, but she is not so much concerned about the external feast as she is eager to see that all proceeds smoothly, that the holy joy is not disturbed. She is anxious to spare the bridal couple embarrassment, and the guests any mortification due to the lack of wine—so important at a wedding feast.

She is the first to notice it: "They have no wine" (John 2:3). Immediately, she thinks of a remedy and intervenes with prayer.

2. Mary has boundless care and solicitude for each of her children. Her prayer is very brief but humble, accompanied by great and most-powerful faith. She is the Mother of Jesus. This is the main reason for her power. In narrating this episode, the gospel calls the virgin: "The mother of Jesus" (cf. John 2:3), three times in the space of five verses.

At first sight it would seem that Jesus' answer is somewhat discouraging: "O woman, what have you to do with me? My hour has not yet come" (John 2:4).

But the Mother of Jesus knows she will be listened to as always. She acts as if the grace is already certain, saying to the servants: "Do whatever he tells you" (John 2:5).

And so the miracle is performed, because, although Jesus' hour has not yet come, Mary's hour has already come—the hour of her intercession.

3. Mary has wisdom to know our necessities, goodness which is moved by our miseries, and power to intercede for us and come to our assistance. This is why we should confide in this Mother.

Her eyes are turned toward all her children, the just and the sinners, in order to discern our spiritual and material needs, difficulties and dangers. She knows them all.

Moreover, she is more sensitive and compassionate than any earthly mother, even the best. She is the Mother of mercy.

Again, she is powerful before the Father, whom she has faithfully served; before the Son, over whom she exercises a type of command; before the Holy Spirit, whose intimate Bride she is.

The consequences of this miracle were much more extensive than merely keeping the wedding guests happy. The Gospel says: "This, the first of his signs, Jesus did at Cana in Galilee, and manifested his glory; and his disciples believed in him" (John 2:11). From this miracle resulted the faith of the disciples, the glory of Jesus, and the first fruits of Jesus' ministry, which was to continue for three years.

Mary leads us to Jesus; she leads souls to Him, and brings Him to souls.

Reflection—Do I have faith in the intercession, goodness and power of Mary? Am I devoted to her? Do I imitate Mary in her thoughtfulness?

Resolution—No day must pass without my praying to Mary to obtain for me a heart full of love for God and neighbor.

Prayer—Remember, O most gracious Virgin Mary, that never was it known that anyone who fled to your protection, implored your help, or sought your intercession, was left unaided. Inspired with this confidence, I fly to you, O Virgin of virgins, my Mother; to you I come, before you I stand, sinful and sorrowful. O Mother of the Word Incarnate! Despise not my petitions, but in your mercy hear and answer me. Amen.

MARY SHARES IN THE SUFFERINGS OF JESUS CHRIST

"When Jesus saw his mother, and the disciple whom he loved standing near, he said to his mother, 'Woman, behold, your son.' Then he said to the disciple, 'Behold, your mother.' And from that hour the disciple took her to his own home."   —John 19:25-27

1. Informed that Jesus had been condemned to death, Mary anxiously joined Him to accompany Him to Calvary. A look of tender love between Mother and Son was enough for mutual understanding and union in sufferings, in intentions and in the

sacrifice. All this was for one and the same purpose: the glory of the Father and the salvation of mankind.

Before Mary's own eyes, Jesus was treated cruelly, stripped of His clothes and nailed to the cross. St. John the Evangelist says: "Standing by the cross of Jesus were his mother, and his mother's sister, Mary the wife of Clopas, and Mary Magdalene" (John 19:25). There were several women, but the Virgin had a very specific purpose: she was the Co-Redemptrix of mankind. She offered her Son; she offered herself. There were two altars on Calvary: the cross for her Son; the heart pierced by a sharp sword for Mary.

2. Calvary is the place where Jesus crushed the serpent's head and snatched the prey from his hands.

There, heaven was reopened to mankind. God was reconciled with man. From the cross came the sacrifice of the new law, the Eucharist and the other sacraments. Because of the cross, souls would again have the life of grace, the Church would be strengthened and all blessings would be bestowed upon humanity. The Holy Trinity was given the greatest glory, worthy praise, sufficient satisfaction and the abundant price for every grace.

Mary was fulfilling her mission: having prepared the Victim and the new Priest, it was now for her to assist Him in the great Sacrifice and to offer Him to the Father. It was the supreme moment predicted in the Scriptures, foreseen by Mary and announced by Jesus.

Mary suffered indescribable pain and her soul was pierced by a sword of sorrow. She suffered with full abandonment to the divine will. More totally than all the saints she lived the words: "Not my will, but Yours be done, O Lord." She did not accuse those who were the cause of her sufferings, nor did she consider her pain too great. She suffered in union with Jesus the Redeemer, sharing His shame and humiliations. She was the Co-redemptrix. She knew this was her mission, and she fulfilled it from Bethlehem to Calvary. She suffered in loving silence, as did Jesus, who went to His death without a murmur. She loved and was silent. She was an example to the holy women, to the Apostles, and to the martyrs of all times.

3. The apostolate of suffering surpasses all others, because it is more intimately associated with the Savior's work and more efficacious before God. This apostolate shows a true and profound love for souls. It is the apostolate of generous souls and of loving hearts. It is also the sure way of sanctification, "If any man would come after me, let him deny himself and take up his cross daily and follow me" (Luke 9:23).

When one loves to the point of accepting sacrifices willingly, there is no doubt that that person is truly with God.

The Sacrifice of Calvary is repeated every day upon our altars: the same Victim, the same principal Offerer, the same purposes. Let us participate at Mass, uniting ourselves to Jesus, Victim and Priest. Let us have the dispositions of Mary at the foot of the cross. She united her sorrow to her Son's. Let us bring some of our sacrifices to unite to the sacrifice of Jesus: our pains, our mortifications and our acts of obedience to the will of God.

Reflection—Do I accept sufferings in union with the sufferings of Jesus and Mary? Do I understand the sacrifice of the Mass? What are my dispositions at Mass?

Resolution—Going to Holy Mass, I shall accompany Jesus and Mary on the way to Calvary and participate in the Mass to immolate myself with Jesus.

Prayer—Sorrowful Virgin, make me more Christian each day, so I may know Jesus, and Him crucified. Grant that I may know how to renounce myself and embrace my daily cross. May my death, accepted for love of Jesus, find me similiar to Him who died for me.

MARY SHARES IN THE JOY OF THE RESURRECTION

"O foolish men, and slow of heart to believe all that the prophets have spoken! Was it not necessary that the Christ should suffer these things and enter into his glory?"
—Luke 24:25-26

1. Mary had participated more fully than the Apostles and disciples in the tremendous drama of the passion of Jesus. Her sorrow was greater; her faith, stronger; her spiritual fruits superabundant. She had seen the ancient prophecies fulfilled one by one, as well as those made by Jesus Himself regarding His passion and death.

Mary was certain that the prophecies regarding the glorious life would also be fulfilled: the Resurrection, the Ascension, the glory of Christ in heaven, His kingdom on earth—the Church.

The adverse winds that shook and extinguished more feeble flames instead made the flame of Mary's faith blaze even more brightly. She awaited the fulfillment in silence and in prayer. Meanwhile, she encouraged and strengthened the confused Apostles: "I will strike the shepherd, and the sheep will be scattered" (Mark 14:27). Mary humbly reunited them around herself in the Cenacle.

2. Because of her faith, Mary did not go to the sepulcher to see her Son again and to embalm His body: she knew and believed that He would rise. The Gospels are silent about this, as they are about many other facts, but tradition and piety hold that the risen Christ appeared first of all to Mary most holy. He had intimately united the Virgin to Himself in the Incarnation, in His life and in His passion. Thus He had to unite her to Himself in the Resurrection, the Ascension, the descent of the Holy Spirit and heaven.

When Jesus had risen, Mary was the first to reap the benefits of this great mystery, by embracing her divine Son once again. She was the first to enjoy the heavenly youthfulness which bloomed anew in the body which she, blessed among women, had given Him. She saw and felt her own body glorified in the glorious body of her most holy Son. She kissed those wounds which were to be the joy of heaven.

Mary reverently adored Jesus risen, as one day she had adored Him as an Infant in the crib, and later as a Victim crucified on Calvary. From that moment her heart was inflamed with a new love; but above all her faith blazed all the more.

3. Supernatural gifts come from God—especially the first one: faith. Acts of faith and prayer increase this great gift. Above all, let us ask for faith in the Last Things; faith in the existence of God; and faith that He is Remunerator; that is, He rewards the good and punishes sinners. Let us ask for faith in the particular judgment, faith in the purpose for which we were created, faith in paradise, faith in the universal judgment, faith in the eternal value of merit, of good works, and of Divine Providence.

Reflection—Am I firm in my faith? Do difficulties and contradictions increase my faith? Do I often think of the Last Things, and are they a guide for my life?

Resolution—I believe in the Resurrection, the Ascension into heaven, and the glory of Jesus Christ. I want to follow Him daily.

Prayer—Blessed Virgin, Mother of the Savior, obtain for me an increase of faith. Jesus did not call you simply to follow Him to Calvary, but He had you take part in the glory of the Resurrection. Grant that I, too, may follow this way in order to arrive at the same glorious resurrection.

MARY, MOTHER OF THE CHURCH

"All these with one accord devoted themselves to prayer, together with the women and Mary the mother of Jesus, and with his brethren."   —Acts 1:14

1. After the Ascension of Jesus into heaven, the Apostles gathered in the Cenacle to pray, reflect and await the Holy Spirit. There were Peter and John, James and Andrew, Philip and Thomas, Bartholomew and Matthew, James the son of Alphaeus,

Simon the Zealot, and Jude, the brother of James. Matthias was elected in place of Judas, the traitor. All of these persevered in prayer with the women and Mary, the Mother of Jesus. When the day of Pentecost arrived, there was suddenly a loud sound from heaven like a violent wind which filled the whole house.

A globe of fire appeared which divided itself into small flames that settled over each one's head. They were all filled with the Holy Spirit, especially Mary most holy whose prayers had hastened the descent of the Holy Spirit.

2. The Holy Spirit infused in them most precious gifts: an increase of faith, hope and charity. Mary's soul was thus even more greatly sanctified. She was a living and constant example to everyone— almost the Gospel incarnate—especially after she had received the Spirit's gifts for her new role as Mother of the Church.

She received the gift of counsel to enlighten the Apostles, the evangelists and the faithful;

the gift of fortitude to sustain, comfort and encourage everyone in the face of difficulties and persecution;

the gift of a profound tenderness for the new Christians, pagans and the erring;

the gift of zeal for all souls redeemed by the blood of Jesus Christ.

She was given a particular light to know the nature, mission and rights of the Church.

She received a most ardent love for the kingdom of Jesus Christ and its extension over the earth.

From then on her prayers were for Peter and for the Twelve. She lived for the Church and carried it in her heart with the same care that she had for her Son, Jesus.

3. The gifts of the Holy Spirit are given to each soul, according to its dispositions and its mission. Let us ask for knowledge, wisdom, understanding, counsel, piety and fear of the Lord.

Above all, let us ask for zeal for the salvation of souls, love of the Church, fortitude, generosity and piety.

Let us ask to be living and active members of the Church.

Reflection—Do I have a true devotion to the Holy Spirit? Do I often ask Him for His gifts? Do I try to increase my faith in the Church? Do I work for her expansion? Her liberty and exaltation?

Resolution—I shall love the Church always more and be her fervent child.

Prayer—O Mary, Mother of the Church, obtain a renewed Pentecost upon the Church, upon her ministers, and upon all apostles. Obtain for her: devoted children, freedom in the exercise of her mission, and unity of her members with the Successor of Peter, the Vicar of Christ.

Daughters of St. Paul

MASSACHUSETTS
50 St. Paul's Ave., Jamaica Plain, Boston, MA 02130; **617-522-8911.**
172 Tremont Street, Boston, MA 02111; **617-426-5464; 617-426-4230.**

NEW YORK
78 Fort Place, Staten Island, NY 10301; **718-447-5071; 718-447-5086.**
59 East 43rd Street, New York, NY 10017; **212-986-7580.**
625 East 187th Street, Bronx, NY 10458; **212-584-0440.**
525 Main Street, Buffalo, NY 14203; **716-847-6044.**

NEW JERSEY
Hudson Mall—Route 440 and Communipaw Ave.,
Jersey City, NJ 07304; **201-433-7740.**

CONNECTICUT
202 Fairfield Ave., Bridgeport, CT 06604; **203-335-9913.**

OHIO
2105 Ontario Street (at Prospect Ave.), Cleveland, OH 44115;
216-621-9427.
616 Walnut Street, Cincinnati, OH 45202; **513-421-5733; 513-721-5059.**

PENNSYLVANIA
1719 Chestnut Street, Philadelphia, PA 19103; **215-568-2638.**

VIRGINIA
1025 King Street, Alexandria, VA 22314; **703-683-1741; 703-549-3806.**

SOUTH CAROLINA
243 King Street, Charleston, SC 29401; **803-577-0175.**

FLORIDA
2700 Biscayne Blvd., Miami, FL 33137; **305-573-1618; 305-573-1624.**

LOUISIANA
4403 Veterans Memorial Blvd., Metairie, LA 70006; **504-887-7631;
504-887-0113.**
423 Main Street, Baton Rouge, LA 70802; **504-343-4057; 504-381-9485.**

MISSOURI
1001 Pine Street (at North 10th), St. Louis, MO 63101; **314-621-0346;
314-231-1034.**

ILLINOIS
172 North Michigan Ave., Chicago, IL 60601; **312-346-4228; 312-346-3240.**

TEXAS
114 Main Plaza, San Antonio, TX 78205; **512-224-8101; 512-224-0938.**

CALIFORNIA
1570 Fifth Ave., San Diego, CA 92101; **619-232-1442.**
46 Geary Street, San Francisco, CA 94108; **415-781-5180.**

WASHINGTON
2301 Second Ave., Seattle, WA 98121; **206-441-3300; 206-441-3210.**

HAWAII
1143 Bishop Street, Honolulu, HI 96813; **808-521-2731.**

ALASKA
750 West 5th Ave., Anchorage, AK 99501; **907-272-8183.**

CANADA
3022 Dufferin Street, Toronto 395, Ontario, Canada.